Economic calculation
and forms of property

Economic calculation and forms of property

by Charles Bettelheim

Translated by John Taylor

Monthly Review Press
New York and London

Copyright © 1975 by Monthly Review Press
All Rights Reserved

Originally published under the title *Calcul économique et formes de propriété* by François Maspero, Paris, France. Copyright © 1970 by Librairie François Maspero.

Library of Congress Cataloging in Publication Data
Bettelheim, Charles.
    Economic calculation and forms of property.
    Translation of Calcul économique et formes de propriété.
    Bibliography: p.
    1. Comparative economics.   2. Marxian economics.   3. Property and socialism.   I. Title.
HB97.5.B39513   335.4'12   74-21473
ISBN 0-85345-360-8

First Printing

Monthly Review Press
62 West 14th Street, New York, N.Y. 10011
21 Theobalds Road, London WCIX 8SL

Manufactured in the United States of America

Contents

Translator's note   vii
Preface   ix

I. Economic calculation and monetary calculation

1. Situating the problem   3
2. The "presence" of commodity categories   28

II. State property, enterprise, and planning

1. State property in social formations in transition
   between capitalism and socialism   71
2. Unit of production and "enterprise"   108
3. Planning and the predominance of state property   130
4. The structures of the processes of production,
   money, and the plan   157

General bibliography   165
Supplementary bibliography   167

Translator's note

In the original French publication of *Calcul économique et formes de propriété,* Bettelheim selected his quotations from the Editions Sociales edition of *Capital.* The first three volumes of this edition, which contain the English volume one of *Capital,* were translated by Roy and proofread by Marx himself. Consequently, in this translation, I have generally preferred to translate the Roy edition, rather than simply relying on the English translation of volume one by Moore and Aveling. So, where quotations are from volume one, I have given references both to the Editions Sociales (1969) and the Progress Publishers (1965) editions. In the case of volumes two and three of *Capital,* the French and English translations from the German are more "orthodox," and here I have simply referred to the Progress Publishers (1966–1967) edition. In a few cases—as Bettelheim himself indicates—these deviate from the German Dietz Verlag edition of Marx and Engels' *Werke.* Quotations from *Theories of Surplus-Value* are, similarly, taken from the English translation of the *Werke,* published by Progress Publishers (1969–1972).

Quotes from *Anti-Dühring* are taken from the 1969 English (Progress Publishers) edition, except where this deviates from the original German edition, in which case I refer to Botigelli's (1950) French translation (Editions Sociales)—the one Bettelheim also uses—which seems to me to be a more rigorous translation.

Finally, quotations from *Economic Problems of Socialism in the USSR* are taken from the new (1972) Chinese translation (Foreign Languages Press, Peking), which is a reprint of the text given in the 1952 English pamphlet of the same name, since this translation adheres more closely to the original than do any other publications of this work presently available.

—John Taylor

Preface

The contents of this book are an extension of previous research, some of which is still being carried on. Consequently, the reader will not find a systematic exposition of bodies of knowledge that have already been produced, whose forms of proof can all be presented, but rather, the exposition of work in progress. This inevitably involves "a return to the past" and the revival of questions that have apparently already been dealt with. The analyses that follow must, therefore, be considered partly provisional.

The aim of this work is twofold: firstly, to put forward and specify a certain number of concepts, in order to open up a discussion that will enable current research to develop more quickly; secondly, to indicate some of the conclusions that can be drawn by using these concepts.

To take this second step: the use of the concepts presented here in a concrete analysis is only outlined in the following pages. Since they were written, the concrete analysis of the Soviet social formation has been continued. Indeed, this task has become urgent, given the problems that the present-day Soviet reality raises. However, these problems can only be dealt with if the meaning of the term "collective ownership of the means of production," is clarified.

When the concepts developed here are inserted into the analysis of the Soviet social formation, they give the question, "Is the Soviet Union socialist?" a precise meaning, as well as enable an answer to be developed.

It is this very question that I hope to answer in a book that will be ready very soon, which will form a concrete analysis, guided and assisted by the concepts put forward here. Therefore, while the following pages have an autonomy of their own, they do constitute a preparation and a complement to this future publication.[1]

The research presented here has a fundamental aim: to produce and to specify the concepts necessary for the analysis of social formations in transition between capitalism and socialism, primarily with the aim of determining the meaning of monetary calculation and economic calculation, as well as the conditions under which the latter can be developed. The pursuit of this objective, in the present state of the problematic, required the coverage of a relatively extensive field. Indeed, it was necessary to be able to account for a whole series of "calculating" and "planning" practices, whose meaning could not be adequately grasped by concepts in their present state of development.

The very order in which various questions are dealt with reveals that the objective initially pursued was much more limited than the one that ultimately had to be aimed at. At the outset, it was simply a question, in line with a step analogous to the one already taken in a previous work,[2] of examining the significance of certain economic practices in the "socialist countries," and the conformity of these practices to the objectives that were sought after. Of particular importance were the practices of "economic calculation" carried out either by the planning organizations or by the enterprises. As is well known, these calculations use "monetary magnitudes" as well as "physical magnitudes"; therefore, they imply the "utilization" of money and commodity categories. The use made of "monetary magnitudes" forced us to raise the question of the meaning of calculations carried out on the basis of these magnitudes; and this all the more so, since the results of these calculations are largely inscribed in advance in the existing price system—a system that is itself a product of commodity relations and political and administrative decisions.

Yet, despite all this, it rapidly became apparent that what was the departure point could only be such in relation to the questions posed, while the answers given to these questions required a long detour.

In order to try and answer the initial questions in a satisfactory way, it seemed indispensable to pose many other questions, concerning the ensemble of the political, economic, and ideological relations in the social formations that were analyzed. As a result, a much more profound research task was imposed than the one that had been anticipated at the outset.

In the course of the work that was subsequently carried out, the concepts that were initially used, and which served as raw material, had to be partially transformed. Most of these original concepts had to undergo a differential treatment because they had been produced in the process of analyzing capitalist social formations; here it was a question of using them in the analysis of social formations in transition between capitalism and socialism.

The process that was begun in this way is far from being achieved. It has forced us to explore a number of closely interrelated themes, especially those corresponding to the concepts of property—possession, holding, unit of production, enterprise, regulation, value-form, monetary and economic calculation, planning, and administration—as well as several others.

It appears that this process has enabled some of these concepts to be developed, and has, therefore, also enabled them to be distinguished from corresponding ideological and descriptive notions; but, to the extent that this process remains unrealized, the results obtained still do not enable us to analyze transitional social formations as complex structures, in which "all the relations co-exist simultaneously and support one another" (according to Marx's expression in the *Poverty of Philosophy*).[3]

It will only be possible to present the concepts in a rigorous order of exposition when the proof of their *combination* and their use in *concrete analyses* has been sustained. Only then will the discourse of the demonstration be able to be "simply the development of the *Gliederung*, of the hierarchised combination of the concepts in the *system* itself."[4]

As I have said, given the present state of this research, such a discourse still cannot be presented.

Consequently, the work undertaken has given rise to a task that is particularly complex. Certainly, this is a result of the profundity of the problems posed, but, as we have seen, it also results from the state of the problematic and the character of the objects we are concerned with: namely, transitional social formations; even more, it is the result of the practices that have developed in these social formations, and of the ideological commentaries that duplicate these practices.

The state of the problematic is characterized, in particular, by the gap separating the theoretical propositions formulated by Marx and Engels on the socialist mode of production from the reality of the "socialist countries." Clearly, it is partly this gap that has compelled us to pose the problems put forward here. The very profundity of the gap has forced us to formulate a series of questions.

These questions, and the answers they invoke, have shown that the gap with which we started off is related, in very general terms, to a double error: theoretical propositions relating to developed socialist social formations have been understood as propositions relating to transitional social formations; reciprocally, every transitional social formation, even if it has abandoned the socialist road, has been identified as a socialist social formation.

Yet, theoretical propositions relating to a developed socialist society cannot be directly used to analyze such *social formations;* it is necessary to elaborate at least the elements of a *theory of transition* from capitalism to socialism.[5]

The object of this theory is the differential elaboration of concepts that enable us to analyze social relations in action and combination, characteristic of the socialist transition of a *concrete social formation* in which this transition has taken place, following from a process of class struggle.

Such a transition implies the presence—either real or possible—of several modes of production or of several systems of relations of production, one of which dominates the others according to modalities that vary over the course of time (determining the specific phases of each *concrete transition*).

What we have said above shows that, beyond the problems posed by possible "errors," research relating to our object encounters a much more substantial difficulty, namely the absence of an *elaborated* theory of social formations in transition between capitalism and socialism.

Certainly, a number of the elements of these theories do exist, either in a form that is already theoretical, or in the practical state. In particular, these elements have been produced when political action in transitional social formations necessitated analyses in the face of concrete (economic, political, and ideological) problems, whose posing and resolution was required by the transition. As a result of this, old concepts have been developed, and new concepts have been produced, yet without it having been possible, up until now, to articulate them in a rigorous theoretical system. This succeeded in giving rise to a considerable number of difficulties, as much at the theoretical as at the political level. In the present situation, an endeavor that aims to determine the field of validity of the available concepts, and to articulate them more rigorously, has become indispensable.

Indeed, such an effort has become all the more indispensable, since a number of practices that profess to be "economic calculation" and "planning" conceal, or at least partly conceal, very different practices. Furthermore, since these practices are duplicated by ideological commentaries that aim to present them as something other than what they really are, one finds oneself in a situation in which, despite theoretical endeavors, one can neither acquire a knowledge of reality, nor transform it.

As you will see, the following analyses, which help to sketch out a line of demarcation between monetary calculation and economic and social calculation, make apparent the necessity, and the possibility, of a "decentralization" of economic planning that is *radically* different from the pseudo-decentralization that is at issue today in the Eastern European countries. This pseudo-decentralization is, in effect, nothing other than the restoration of "market mechanisms," thereby implying the renunciation of socialist planning. You will also see that the content of this planning is partly obscured by the extreme centralization of the state. This centralization, which derives from a hypertrophy of the state apparatus, ultimately acts as an obstacle to a social domination of production and contributes to the reinforcement of the role of monetary and commodity relations.

In the text which follows, *the analysis of the problems of the overall social unity* peculiar to social formations in transition between capitalism and socialism will not be developed. We will only develop the analysis of *some of these problems*—those that are concerned primarily with the *economic level* of these social formations. Consequently, relations that are other than economic will be indicated but not made the object of a systematic examination.

To sum up: The questions that invoked the existence of two forms of "economic calculation" were discovered to be precisely those that enabled the particular complexity of social formations in transition between capitalism and socialism to be made apparent; hence, the research that follows had to be involved in many different directions. For the same reasons, this research only forms a preliminary to the specific examination of the problems of economic calculation. These problems will have to be made the object of a subsequent text.

—Paris, July 1969

Notes

1. Since the editing of this text, it has already become apparent that it requires a certain number of "corrections"; however, this process remains unfinished, and it seemed preferable to publish it in its present state precisely in order to subject it to discussion, rather than to try and insert these "corrections" into it.
2. Charles Bettelheim, *La Transition vers l'économie socialiste* (Paris: Maspero, 1968).
3. Karl Marx, *The Poverty of Philosophy* (Moscow: Progress Publishers, 1966), p. 96.
4. Louis Althusser, Etienne Balibar, et al., *Reading Capital* (New York: Pantheon, 1970; London: New Left Books, 1970), p. 68.
5. Some of the problems raised here were approached in my book, *La Transition vers l'économie socialiste.*

Part I

Economic calculation
and monetary calculation

Chapter 1

Situating the problem

The problem that we intend to analyze is that of "economic calculation" in social formations in transition between capitalism and socialism. This problem appears to be related both to that of planning and to the conditions for the circulation of products. The point of departure for our analysis is formed by a number of theoretical propositions relating to economic calculation and to the plan in a socialist society. We will compare these propositions with actual practices in transitional social formations.

1. A text of Engels

We will begin with the well-known text of *Anti-Dühring*. In this work, Engels tackles the problem of the conditions necessary for the formulation of a plan of production in a socialist society.

With regard to this society, which has taken "possession of the means of production and uses them in production that is directly socialised,"[1] Engels writes:

> Direct social production and direct distribution preclude all exchange of commodities, therefore also the transformation of the products into commodities . . . and consequently also their transformation into *values*.[2]

It is on the basis of this proposition that Engels describes his conception of economic calculation in such a society:

> The quantity of social labour contained in a product need not then be established in a roundabout way; daily experience shows in a direct way

3

how much of it is required on the average. Society can simply calculate how many hours of labour are contained in a steam-engine, a bushel of wheat of the last harvest, or a hundred square yards of cloth of a certain quality. . . . Hence, on the assumptions we made above, society will not assign values to products. It will not express the simple fact that the hundred square yards of cloth have required for their production, say, a thousand hours of labour in the oblique and meaningless way, stating that they have been the *value* of a thousand hours of labour. It is true that even then it will be necessary for society to know how much labour each article of consumption requires for its production. It will have to arrange its plan of production in accordance with its means of production, which include, in particular, its labour-power. The useful effects of the various articles of consumption, compared with one another and with the quantities of labour required for their production, will in the end determine the plan. People will be able to manage everything very simply, without the intervention of much-vaunted "value." [3]

COMMENTS

Note that in this text, Engels is talking about labor-time actually carried out, and not socially necessary labor-time (this is a problem that we will have to return to later). Note also that, in another connection, Marx stressed that the place given to calculation of labor in time (or in quantity) corresponds to a particular level of development of the productive forces. On this point, see the analyses that Marx devoted to the effects of the development of the machine industry, particularly in the *Grundrisse*.[4]

This text can be the departure point for a whole series of reflections, but, for the moment, I don't propose to develop all of these. I will only concentrate on the points which, from now on, we must focus on. These correspond to two types of problems:

1. Those which arise from a comparison of the preceding *text* of Engels (as they could arise from a comparison of a number of Marx's and Engels' texts) with the *practice* of socialist planning.

2. Those that provoke an investigation of some of the above formulations.

2. Engels' text and the practice of socialist planning

According to Engels' propositions, the categories of value and price *do not have to intervene* in the calculations necessary for socialist planning. These calculations must be based upon the comparison of the "useful effects" of use objects in themselves and in relation to the quantities of labor necessary for their production. We know that this expectation of Engels is apparently unrealized in any of the present-day socialist economies. Economic calculations are not directly made in labor-time in any of these social formations. They always seem to be carried out, at least to a large extent, through commodity categories, even though economic plans (when formulated according to "social" or "political" priorities) do take into account elements other than those that enter into "monetary calculations" in the evaluation of "costs" expressed in money.

(a) Monetary calculations

Such "costs" are not, in any way, the result of "measurement" (in the same way that one can speak of *measuring* operations in the natural sciences). They are simple *magnitudes of accounting*, the dimensions of which are spontaneously given through a system of prices. Sometimes this system appears to be "produced by the market," while at other times it seems to be the result of administrative or statutory decisions. But this changes nothing with regard to the *given* character of prices. Again, this character remains unmodified by the use of anticipated prices, that is, future or planned prices, since at no time does measurement intervene, but only *accounting operations*, which can be more or less complex, real or fictitious, and related to the present or future. Consequently, economic calculations carried out under such conditions are only *monetary or accounting calculations*. Therefore, for the simple convenience of exposition, and because of the functions that these calculations fulfill, they will eventually be denoted by the term "monetary economic calculation"; this term ought thereby to remain faithful to the reality it refers to.

What we have said so far implies that there necessarily exists a radical break between any form of *monetary calculation* and *economic calculation;* the latter refers either to the *measurement* of costs of more or less useful labor, or even to the social utility of different types of production or activities. Calculation in money refers to a unit of accounting, that is, *in fact,* to a unit that effectively intervenes in *exchanges,* thereby testifying to the existence of commodity categories and the value-form.

COMMENTS

No doubt we can envisage the existence of a unit of accounting that would not intervene in exchanges, but then we mean one of two things. Either it is effectively a question of an *accounting* unit playing the same *accounting* role as that of money, without referring to social relations—in this case, the social function of such an accounting could only be very limited; or else this unit is in reality a unit of *measurement,* and the nature of this measurement, as with the procedures that correspond to it, must be theoretically defined (otherwise nothing is measured) by reference to social equivalents. Such a unit would no longer be a currency, and the magnitudes expressed in this unit *would no longer be prices.* At this point, the question of the possibility of formalizing the evaluation of social units, so that a real unit of measurement can be defined, remains open.

There has often been a temptation to settle the problems posed by the existence of the *value-form* within social formations considered to be socialist—and, therefore, of the contradiction between this and a number of Marx and Engels' propositions (such as the one cited above)—by referring to the category of "survival." In effect, it is sometimes said that there is a "survival" of commodity categories in contemporary social formations. This, of course, does not explain anything; a phenomenon cannot, in itself, be explained by giving it a name, and the present is not explained by a simple reference to the past.

The problem must therefore be examined in itself. This is of considerable importance for us. If social and political priorities, social objectives, etc. are taken into account simultaneously with calculations made in money, this means that actual economic practice is concerned with the *interrelation of two types of economic calculation:* monetary calculation and nonmonetary calculation. The first, in general, conceals the second and tends in appearance to engulf it, making it play a subordinate role to monetary calculation.

(b) The interrelation of the two types of economic calculation

What is meant by the term interrelation, used above, is the following: On the one hand, in the actual practice of "socialist countries," a set of calculations is made that takes into account actual (or eventual) *monetary costs* and *receipts.* It is the totality of these calculations that has been called "monetary calculation" above. The *financial* meaning of such calculation is relatively clear: the *economic* meaning is much less clear, particularly because the conclusions that one can draw from such calculations are strictly dependent on the system of prices. However, this system of prices is always called upon to fulfill a *multitude of functions* (including the functions of redistribution of revenues between units of production, incentives, or restraint on the use of such and such a product, etc.), so that the meaning of calculations made in terms of such prices (particularly from the viewpoint of setting up a plan designed for several years) remains extremely dubious (since with other prices, one could arrive at different conclusions).[5]

On the other hand, in the practice of "socialist countries," nonmonetary calculations—that is, a set of operations that are still very feebly formalized—are made that aim to take into consideration the requirements of enlarged reproduction, social and political priorities, and, in the final analysis, the social utility and social costs of different types of production or activities.

Theoretically, it seems that a real social domination of the process of the development of the productive forces and of the transformation of relations of production implies that this second type of calculation (or social economic calculation = SEC) must play a role on its own (as Engels' formulation suggests), or must, at least, play a dominant role. In actual economic practice, it seems that it is usually the opposite that occurs. monetary calculation playing a dominant role, and SEC only playing a subordinate or auxiliary role under the form of corrections to the conclusions drawn from the former.

In what follows in our analysis, we will have to investigate the reason for this duality of economic calculations and for the prevalence, at least in appearance, of monetary calculations; but, first of all, we must return to a number of Engels' propositions.

3. The meaning of some of Engels' formulations

Engels' text contains a number of formulations that we must particularly concentrate on.

(a) The "useful effects" of different use objects

Firstly, we should note Engels' proposition where he speaks of the need to compare the "useful effects" of various use objects and relates them to the quantities of labor necessary for their production in order to determine the content of the plan. This formulation raises problems of decisive importance for economic calculation.

We shall have to come back to these problems later on and, in particular, specify the content of the concept socially necessary labor-time (or quantity), which is a fundamental concept for economic calculation; but for the moment, I will limit myself to formulating a number of remarks on these various points.

If Engels' proposition is interpreted rigorously, it will be concluded that in socialist society, people must *provide themselves with the means for comparing the socially useful effects of different objects* and for relating them to the quantities of labor necessary for their production. Herein lies the *necessity* for the establishment of a plan.

In effect, at the level of the physical properties of different objects, their "useful effects" cannot be compared, still less weighed against each other and related to quantities of labor. In the space of their physical properties, the various use objects are, in general, radically different from each other. Thus Marx was able to show in the first few pages of *Capital* that in this "space," one cannot claim to measure and directly compare the *useful effects* of different objects.

Consequently, if Engels speaks of such a comparison, what he has in mind is not the physical properties but the *socially useful effects* of different objects.

It is, therefore, the latter that must be compared. This comparison requires the construction of theoretical space within which the measurement of the socially useful effects of objects can be carried out, and where the quantities of socially necessary labor required to produce them can also be measured.

Comments on the measurement of "useful effects"

A problem is posed, therefore, which is not yet fully resolved. Nevertheless, its theoretical nature is analogous to that of a number of other problems to which the development of the sciences has provided a solution. It is a question of producing the concepts *that enable the socially useful effects of different types of production to be measured.*

In effect, all measurement requires the production of the concept of what is measured. Such a concept, as a necessary preliminary to measurement itself, can only be produced from within a conceptual system, that is, a theory that gives measurement its meaning. Measurement, therefore, cannot be an isolated process but is a moment *in the process of production of scientific concepts*, and from this, it passes into *scientific experimentation*, which is its specific form. (This clearly does not mean that scientific experimentation can only produce something measurable.)

If there can be an illusion that *calculation* could be substituted for *measurement*, it is because, as a general rule (in physics, for example), experimentation does not directly deliver a measurement. It delivers indices of material indicators, *the variations of which enable the magnitudes that are measured to be calculated.* But this calculation, which takes up a position above or below experimentation, is only possible because the *conceptual* system from within which calculation operates has been constructed.[6] It will clearly have to be reconstructed or refounded if the quantitative results that lead to calculations carried out on the basis of observed variations are in contradiction with what theory would suggest.

This short reminder is indispensable, due to the confusion that surrounds the notion of economic calculation when this term is used to designate a *monetary calculation*, that is, a calculation that does not depend on *measured* but upon *given*[7] magnitudes. It demonstrates that measurement is always the result of a *process of abstraction that, from its inception, totally eliminates* "qualities." Consequently—and it is on this basis that the still unresolved problem must be posed—if qualitatively different "useful effects" can be *compared* and *measured*, it is by abstracting from their qualitative diversity.[8]

Clearly, this abstraction can only result in effective measurements if the "useful effects" are of objects that are theoretically measurable, that is, if they are not simply qualitatively different, thereby having the traits of a quantitative abstraction. If they possess such traits, it is *because they are inscribed in a socially organized production and consumption;* this is their common trait, from which the concept of their *measurement* can be constructed.

The road that leads to this construction takes into account along its route the *substitutability* of labor and its products. This is because this substitutability is *socially determined*, in its feasibility and in its quantitative characteristics (and also, therefore, in its limits), by the effective insertion of this labor and its products into a *real social space*, in which at one time it may fulfill equivalent, and at another complementary, functions.

In the same way that the *value-form* refers to a particular type of substitutability (through the intermediary of *exchanges*, and hence of determinate relations of production), the *form of the plan* similarly refers to another type of substitutability. The latter replaces the value-form and causes it to disappear when the *objective conditions* are realized, for this substitutability to be the object of an *effective measurement*, and not just of an evaluation or adjustment (which has actually happened).[9] Without a doubt, this presupposes the full development of new relations of production, and, within the framework of the latter, a further progress in the *socialization of the productive forces*.

COMMENTS

Within the framework of capitalist relations of production, the most developed form of commodity relations, social labor assumes the form of private labor. The latter only asserts its social character through exchange. It is only through this exchange that the *social labor-time necessary for the production* of various commodities (and it is this time that constitutes the theoretical space to which the analysis of prices refers) manifests—and at the same time conceals—itself under the *value-form*. It is only because social labor can be understood here in the abstraction of its concept (naive observation only reveals labor as private, isolated, or separated) that it can be called "abstract labor."

Once socialist relations of production are fully developed, the contradiction "social/private" labor disappears, and objective conditions are created for social labor to manifest itself under a form other than that of the value-form. Nevertheless, as with all forms, the value-form must be analyzed in order that the relations it conceals can be brought to light and concepts adequate to the measurement of social labor can be constructed. This social labor is never directly given in the space of physical labor (whose duration is measured chronometrically) since it is precisely a question here of the space of *social* labor; and the time of labor "socially necessary" for production is only under exceptional circumstances the labor-time *that is effectively devoted to it*.

It is now necessary to raise the following problem: if, in the capitalist mode of production (CMP), the quantity of socially necessary labor-time is the measure of value (and hence the socially necessary labor, the *theoretical space* to which the analysis of prices refers), then the "social necessity" implied in the concept of socially necessary labor is that of the *appropriation of surplus-labor*. It is the latter that is the very object of the CMP, while the satisfaction of needs or of demand is only a means. Consequently, in the CMP, the social utility or the socially useful effect of the various forms of labor only manifest themselves through their capacity to produce surplus-value or to assist in its production or increase (hence the "rationality" of the profit criterion for the CMP).[10]

When the CMP gives way to the socialist mode of production (SMP), or even when socialist relations of production *dominate* capitalist relations of production in a transitional social formation, the object of production is no longer the appropriation of surplus-value but the satisfaction of social needs. From this moment, *theoretical space* is no longer that of value and prices but of the "useful effects" of labor, and thus of *social utility*. The concept of "socially necessary labor" takes on a radically different meaning here from the one it has in the CMP. Its measurement is now not the surplus-value produced (or the relation of surplus to necessary labor), but the "social utility" produced by the various types of labor. This utility itself varies according both to the proportions into which these labors are constituted, and the social and material conditions within which they take place. Having said this, we still have to elaborate the system of concepts and procedures that enable social utility—of different labors and products, supplied in determinate concrete conditions—to be measured so that the distribution of labor (i.e., of social labor) between the different types of production can be regulated on the basis of this measurement.[11]

At the present moment, various suggestions have been put forward in the direction indicated above, but they have been made in a more or less blind fashion, since the nature of the problem that we are trying to resolve only begins to be posed clearly as a result of the slow progress we are making in solving the problem of "social economic calculation."

Several obstacles to the development of economic calculation

The slowness of this progress is explained by a series of reasons, some objective and others subjective.

1. *The objective reasons*

These are of two types. The first relates to the relatively feeble development of the productive forces in social formations presently in transition from capitalism to socialism. This low level of development results in the continued existence of commodity forms of the economy. (We will come back to this question later on.)

The second objective reason is related to the specific nature of the relations of production that exist in transitional social formations since some of these relations necessarily double commodity relations. (This is another point to which we will return later in the text.)

The existence of market relations is, therefore, doubly determined. Yet the market has the property of operating spontaneously and, according to laws that are specific to it, of bringing the products of different activities into relation with one another. Thus the market produces the appearance of "monetary magnitudes" that seem to lead to an economic calculation. But the latter is, in fact, only a *monetary calculation.*

The presence of these magnitudes and the possibility of more or less "adjusting" them (under the form of planned prices, which take little account of the various social and political evaluations), constitute an obstacle to the development of a theory of the measurement of "useful effects," just as they do to the development of a real *social economic calculation* (SEC).

The objective possibility of a recourse to these spontaneously given "magnitudes" through the implementation of market prices, or of prices derived from market prices, has meant that—in spite of the contradictions inherent in the use of such prices—the necessity of a social economic calculation, in the real sense, has hardly been felt.

This necessity did appear several years ago in the Soviet Union, but in an extremely ambiguous and contradictory fashion, in, for instance, the attempts at "economic calculation" made by V. S. Nemtchinov and V. V. Novozhilov.[12]

These attempts are ambiguous because they do not establish the fundamental distinction that is asserted between *economic* and *monetary* calculation, and they are contradictory because they try to combine the two types of calculation. Even less do they provide a point of departure for any reflection on this subject, since their attempts have been *contaminated* by nonscientific ideological conceptions and, furthermore, *stifled* by the development of commodity relations in the Soviet Union and other "socialist" countries. This development has given a new impetus to the illusion that prices could serve as the basis for a real economic calculation.

COMMENTS

In effect, we are dealing here with an illusion since *economic calculation* only exists if the calculation of economic magnitudes and, consequently, a theoretical *knowledge* of these magnitudes, is dominant. However, calculation carried out on the basis of *prices* is a calculation that is *ignorant* of this basis on which it rests, with the result that it treats *accounting magnitudes* as if they were economic magnitudes. Thus, in terms of the distinction made earlier, simple monetary and financial calculations are carried out under the name of "economic calculation."

In this way, the *monetary cost* of a particular product or a number of products can be calculated clearly: one can also calculate how to reduce this *monetary cost to a minimum* (on the basis of certain hypotheses). Equally, calculations can be undertaken that aim to *maximize* monetary profit in anticipation of a given investment (under particular conditions, including those relative to a system of *prices* and thus also to a system of *wages*). Such calculations are of great importance (they are even essential) for the agents of capital, since they concern the increment in the value of invested funds. Yet these agents have no direct knowledge of the requirements for the development of socialist relations of production or for improvements in the working and living conditions of workers. Economists and econometricians have had to display a naive ingenuity in imagining that monetary calculations can lead to "conclusions" other than those relating to the increment in the value of capital, and particularly in pretending that the means for determining an "economic optimum" can be drawn from these calculations. Besides, this notion can only have an extremely vague content when economically contradictory interests exist: at best, it can designate the system of productive combinations which, within a given structure of prices, wages, and techniques could permit the maximization of the aggregate surplus-value that capital can extract from the exploitation of labor-power.

In reality, the problem mentioned above contains a multitude of implications. At the practical level, it signifies that in transitional social formations, as they have functioned up until now, *historically given market prices* have existed. "Economic calculations," which are really only *monetary* calculations, have been and are carried out with the assistance of these market prices, which, although progressively modified according to various exigencies, are not "thought" and elaborated as a coherent and specific system.

COMMENTS

Obviously, a very important problem here is the following: what are the *objective laws* that determine *actual prices* and also, therefore, the relations between prices in transitional social formations? At the present stage of theoretical development it is very difficult to formulate a reply to this question, basically for two reasons:

(a) In these social formations, the relations between actual prices do not depend solely upon the economic level; they are, at least in part, directly determined by the political level and, more generally, by "politics," that is, by the *class struggle*.

On the contrary, in competitive capitalism, the level of prices is *directly* determined by the economic level. This means that the other levels—the ideological and political—generally operate in a way that is mediate and hidden under the apparent form of "objective economic laws." The latter are all the more easily thought to be "inescapable" because the social and political constraints that these levels assign to the economic are not manifest as such.

Under conditions of monopoly capitalism, the political level intervenes much more directly and visibly in the relations between actual prices; nevertheless, the latter are *in appearance* still essentially determined by the economic level.

Consequently, while the system of prices can be thought of as being fundamentally determined by "economic laws" in capitalist social formations, this is no longer possible in social formations in transition between capitalism and socialism. Here the objective laws that determine prices *are laws that are visibly dependent* on both the economic and political levels. The intervention of the political is particularly manifest in the "fixing" of "economic objectives," which ought generally to be associated with a system of politically determined prices.

(b) The result of this is that, in transitional social formations, where a more or less large number of prices is either planned or, at least, administratively "fixed," prices *seem* to depend on the "decisions" of planning authorities, since the latter modify historically given prices. However, in order to be compatible both with the requirements of reproduction and with planning objectives (at all levels, and consequently at the level of the strategic objectives of classes) these decisions cannot continually be "arbitrary." Consequently, the constraints that are imposed on such decisions express the objective laws of both the economic and, directly, the political levels concomitantly. Thus, these prices are also determined by *objective social laws.* That these laws determine prices through decisions should no more conceal their objective character than the fact that in a capitalist economy the determination of prices by objective laws and not by "buyers" and "sellers" is never apparent on the surface.[13]

However, given that in this latter case the pressure of objective laws *makes itself felt directly* on these buyers and sellers *at the economic level*, the notion of prices being determined by the "market" or by "competition" is one that emerges from current economic practice. Clearly, it is an illusory notion because *the market does not determine anything.* It is simply the imaginary place where the exigencies of the law of value, and consequently of enlarged reproduction (ER) of the material and social conditions of production, are imposed. It is the imaginary place where the practices of economic agents are ultimately sanctioned when they do not conform to the requirements of ER.

In transitional economies (TE), the illusion that the market "determines prices" has partially disappeared—to the extent that market relations *are not dominant.* The apparent sanction that the market seems to impose on economic agents whose practices are incompatible both with the requirements for enlarged reproduction and the objectives of the plans has as a consequence also disappeared. Yet this lack of respect for the market, when it is presented under the modality of badly planned prices, produces, due to the nature of the relations of production (i.e., the social forms of ownership of the means of production, whether they are collective or under state control), diffuse effects whose influence can be delayed.

The diffuse character of the effects produced by prices drawn up in contradiction with the objectives of the plan (that is, in contradiction with the political objectives themselves) means that these effects do not necessarily appear at the level of all, or some, of the units of production. Generally, they can and do make themselves felt at the level of the overall social formation, for example, in the form of an exacerbation of class contradictions, or of disequilibriums between the development of the different branches of the economy, or by a slowing down in the development of the productive forces, etc.

This empirical practice has, in fact, been possible because commodity categories continue to exist and exercise sufficient pressure for the imposition of a *relatively* "coherent" system of prices, together with the objective requirements of enlarged reproduction as they appear through market exchange, *and* a totality of "objectives" that also depend, at least partly, on these exchanges themselves. It is for this reason that monetary calculation has been able to appear as not entering into contradiction with the initial development of economic calculation that was able to take place.

Therefore, the necessity for constructing the *theoretical framework* for a calculation *independent of the market*, and for formulating social utilities and exigencies has, as yet, hardly been felt—precisely because the market and commodity categories have continued to function. With the increasing socialization of the productive forces,[14] this necessity becomes more and more evident since the objective conditions for the functioning of commodity categories decline in the large sectors of the economy.[15] Thus, the reference points that provide the basis for the functioning (and even the control) of the market also disappear. Market prices, even when they are more or less modified, cease to be "usable" because, for example, the conclusions arrived at from calculations made on the basis of these prices are in *contradiction* with the developmental needs of the overall social formation.

These contradictions can be so visible that, without having need of any theory, one is compelled to refuse to consider calculations in market prices or calculations derived from the market since it is obvious that, in practical terms, they do not signify anything.

Thus, the fact that the products of particular activities have *overall social effects* (for example, such activities as education, scientific research, public health, and also, increasingly, various branches of production whose development profoundly modifies the general conditions of production and consumption such as transport, electricity, electronics, etc.) consequently means that the "price" at which the products of these activities can be sold on the market (even if some of them are actually sold) is visibly deprived of meaning.

This "loss of signification" by the prices at which particular products can, or could, be sold on the market *affects capitalist production itself.* Given a particular level of socialization of the productive forces, the price mechanism can no longer function for a part of capitalist production; hence, there develops "nonprofitable production," political subsidization, and the recourse to monetary calculation, resulting in the intervention of other prices than market prices.

Yet, within the framework of the CMP, the system of prices is invested with such ideological power and, furthermore, fulfills such important functions in the distribution of surplus-value and in the class struggle (wage demands being seen as opposing the "requirements of profitability") that "market prices" appear as "normal prices"; thus, when the latter are not given spontaneously, an inquiry is necessarily undertaken into what they "ought to be."

In transitional social formations, the loss of signification by market prices that accompanies the socialization of the productive forces is clearly as considerable as it is in capitalist social formations. Moreover, given a particular level of socialization of these forces, the pursuit of monetary calculations appears to be related not only to ideological reasons but also to the effects of class relations. This pursuit is accompanied by the deepening of the contradictions inherent in monetary calculation.

As long as these contradictions are relatively feeble, they can be overcome by empirical means, but this is no longer possible when they become intensified. Then it is necessary either to retrace one's steps theoretically and politically or to give up the particular political objectives and planned relations that the realization of these steps requires. Naturally, such a renunciation is not imposed mechanically but is overdetermined by the effects of the class struggle, that is, by the efforts of those social classes that benefit from the development of commodity relations and whose aim is the imposition of such relations.

2. Subjective reasons

To the objective (and for the moment dominant) reasons for the slow progress achieved in the field of SEC must be added, it seems, subjective—or rather, ideological—reasons. These can be presented under at least two essential aspects:

(a) Marx's theory of value is built upon a radical critique of every explanation of *exchange-value in terms of* "use-value." Yet many Marxist economists have thought it possible to conclude from this critique that economic calculation could or ought to "abstract from" use-value. This is untenable, precisely because *economic calculation* is developed in an *area other than that of value and prices*.

(b) The second aspect of these ideological difficulties is of the same type. Since the end of the nineteenth century, Marxists have had to carry out a systematic and scientifically indispensable critique of marginal utility theories, due to the latters' ideological premises. This critique was directed at the use made of "calculation on a marginal basis" by the supporters of subjective theories of value. As a result, a double sliding has been accomplished here. On the one hand, there has been an attempt to apply critiques founded at the level of the *theory of value* to certain forms of *social economic calculation;* on the other hand, critiques addressed to "marginalism" have been generalized to all calculations carried out on a marginal basis. This last "sliding" can only lead to an impasse since calculation "on a marginal basis" is nothing other than *differential calculation*, which it is impossible to do without. Besides, in the theory of ground rent, Marx himself pointed out some of the conditions under which this calculation should be used.

(b) The "simplicity" of calculations

In the text cited at the beginning of this chapter, Engels insists that the problems involved in drawing up a plan will be settled very simply without the intervention of "value."

We must not be misled by this formulation. It is true that the elimination of the value-form—which makes relations of production appear as relations between things—enables problems to be settled much more directly than they could be through commodity categories. However, this lesser degree of complexity and, therefore, this greater simplicity does not mean that the operations necessary for the formulation of a plan can be carried out easily.

Without anticipating developments to come later in the text, it is useful to recall that even the socialization of the productive forces that already characterizes the capitalist economy means that almost every product is the *result of the labor of the whole society*—and not only of that laborer, or collective labor, who has materially manufactured it, that is, the hands from which the product has come. In effect, the work of the last laborer is performed on objects that have themselves already been transformed by a number of other laborers. This work implies the coincidence of a considerable number of other labors (for the provision of objects and means of labor, together with subsidiary means) that are combined within a highly complex social organization.[16] Furthermore, in large modern enterprises, as for example in the large-scale chemical industry, it is generally impossible to isolate the labor-time necessary for one particular product. Most production is the result of collective labor, which *simultaneously* produces a great variety of products, so that the calculation of the time devoted to supplying *each* of these products cannot be "directly measured" but requires an analysis and a series of complex operations.

At the present moment, most products are the result of extremely diverse activities: extractive and energy-producing industries, chemical, iron and steel, transport, machine-producing industries, etc. This is why the problem of "attributing" a *quantity of labor to a determinate product* or category of products as being the labor used up in *producing* that product is, along with a number of other problems, one that is not easily soluble.

Besides, in a market economy, this problem does not have to be resolved. In this economy, every product has a price, and although the latter is determined (in the last instance and through a series of fluctuations and transformations) by the labor-time socially necessary for its production, no one has to *calculate* this time. The "regulation" of prices by labor-time is the result of a complex social process, which asserts itself forcibly through the fluctuations of the market. The only thing that preoccupies the mind of every capitalist is the relation between cost-price (which is a sum of *monetary expenditures*)[17] and selling-price. Only a theoretical analysis enables us to understand that socially necessary labor-time ultimately regulates prices. But if a theoretical analysis makes possible the formulation of the concept of "socially necessary labor-time," this *theoretical* concept does not, in itself, make the *empirical measurement* of this time possible.

If the quantity of social labor necessary to obtain each category of products (taken individually) cannot be directly verified, it is primarily because the knowledge of this quantity requires not only specific calculating techniques (in particular, making use of analyses based on tables of intersectoral relations) but also and above all, the precise formulation of the "quantity of labor-time socially necessary" in capitalist society and in social formations in transition to socialism.

However, while this concept refers to the conditions of extraction of surplus-value and its distribution among the different fractions of social capital in the capitalist mode of production, it refers to something entirely different under conditions of domination of socialist relations of production. It refers to the "socially useful effects" of different labors. These are no longer dominated by the requirements for the enlarged reproduction of capital, as in the CMP, but by the requirements of a social domination by producers over the conditions of their production and consumption. Thus, it is only on the basis of a transformation of the concept of "quantity of socially necessary labor" that it will be possible to define procedures for the measurement of this quantity. At the present moment, this problem is far from being resolved, and it is useful to emphasize once again that its solution requires the realization of objective conditions, namely a real domination of socialist relations over commodity relations of production, and thus a degree of transformation adequate for transitional social formations.

The fact that the problem of the measurement of socially necessary labor-time is not yet rigorously resolved does not prevent planned economies from functioning effectively, precisely because this functioning implies a considerable recourse to calculations carried out with the assistance of commodity categories, that is, to a *monetary calculation* (which I have also called an "indirect economic calculation"). This being the case, it must never be forgotten that *such a calculation is not a real economic calculation*, and, therefore, that it can only provide indirect and limited indications as to the social utility of such and such an activity, production, or investment. If this is forgotten, one can be led into serious errors.[18] We will see later on what this state of things implies for economic planning.

4. *A summary of the obstacles*
to social economic calculation

In the transitional period, or at least in the early stages of this period, there exist two categories of obstacles to the development of social economic calculation, in the way that Engels had foreseen it.

The first and most fundamental category of obstacles is related to the as yet relatively feeble development of socialist relations of production and of the productive forces corresponding to them. Consequently, the obstacles are related as much to the unevenness of these forces as to the existence of a world capitalist market.[19] The result of this situation is what has been called the "survival" of the value-form. Consequently, the latter is not a survival, but a *presence*—of determinate relations of production—that will be analyzed later.

The second category of obstacles plays a subordinate role; it is related to the inadequate elaboration of the *content* of economic calculation.

Certainly, the *principles* of this calculation, the way in which it ought to intervene in a developed socialist society, have been posed (particularly in the text commented on above); however, as we have just seen, the *precise content* of this calculation remains in part to be defined.

At the time Engels wrote this text, there could be no question, for him, of going beyond the formulation of principles, since he always quite rightly refused to "keep the pots of the future boiling."

Of these two categories of obstacles that are opposed to social economic calculation, the second, as we have seen, is closely subordinated to the first; at the level of knowledge, the second is the consequence of the first. However, this does not mean that the precise formulation of the content of social economic calculation is only made possible by the *complete disappearance of objective obstacles* to the full development of this calculation. In effect, the development and even the recessions of transitional social formations today enable the problem of economic calculation to be posed more explicitly than was previously possible; as a result, we can also begin to define the problematic of this calculation.

If this is the case, it is because, as we have noted repeatedly, one sees *in practice* an intimate intermingling of two types of calculation: a monetary and a nonmonetary calculation. This, as yet, is only in its infancy, but these beginnings are already sufficient for theoretical analysis to take hold of them in order to specify their content and precise forms.

In order to undertake this analysis (which has, as yet, only been outlined here) we must examine more closely the two types of calculation that exist in present-day transitional social formations. In this way we will see both what the relations are that they support, and the differences which separate them. The first question we must examine is that of the relations of production whose existence is signaled by the *presence* of commodity categories.

Notes

1. See "Translator's note," p. 7, for the sources of *Anti-Dühring* quotations. (Trans.)
2. Friedrich Engels, *Anti-Dühring*, 5th ed. (Moscow: Progress Publishers, 1969), p. 366.
3. Ibid., p. 367.
4. Karl Marx, *Grundrisse*, trans. Martin Nicolaus (New York: Vintage Books, 1973).
5. With regard to this, Gregory Grossman's attempt [see "Gold and the Sword: Money in the Soviet Command Economy," in *Industrialization in Two Systems: Essays in Honor of Alexander Gershenkron*, ed. M. Rosovsky (New York: 1966)] to distinguish between a "passive" and an "active" money, the first characterizing the Soviet, and the second the Western capitalist economies, does not get us very far. Since the transcription of the various physical quantities of products into monetary units is not

purely an intellectual exercise but serves as a guide to action (i.e., to decisions), money cannot be said to be "passive"; according to the code used for this transcription (i.e., according to the system of prices), such and such an action will appear as economically rational or justified. It immediately becomes clear that there can be no question of the "passivity" of money when we see the intervention of such notions as monetary costs, recovery period (of invested sums of money), or monetary profitability.

6. In other words, the problem of measurement can only be posed in the determinate process of production of *theoretical knowledge;* it is, therefore, always distinct from the practice of calculation.

7. As we know, the strange phenomenon of a magnitude that is "spontaneously given" (the commodity which has a price), in the absence of any scientific concept of that which it is a magnitude of, was dealt with at great length by Marx at the beginning of *Capital*, where he provided an answer to this question.

8. In the same way, when one wants to *measure* the temperatures of different objects, one *abstracts from* their form, color, density, etc. These, in relation to the object of measurement, are only "qualities." Against this, the *concept* of temperature must be posed and the determinate process of its measurement must be defined.

As Marx recalls in the first few pages of *Capital*, elementary geometry similarly resolves the problem of the measurement of the areas of all rectilinear figures by *abstracting* from the diversity of their forms:

"In order to measure and compare the areas of all rectilinear figures, we decompose them into triangles. But the area of the triangle itself is expressed by something totally different from its visible figure, namely, by half the product of the base into the altitude." (*Capital*, 1:37; *Le Capital*, 1:53) (In their translation, Moore and Aveling render "measure" as "calculate."—Trans.)

It is due to this double operation of *reduction* and *deduction* that the most diverse figures are expressed in "something" common, and are measured in relation to this common "something" that corresponds to a "concept" of the area.

9. The physical sciences also experience a stage in their development at which it is necessary for them to limit themselves to an "adjustment." Thus, temperatures were "adjusted" (graded as more or less) before classical thermodynamics, and then statistics, enabled temperature to be

measured (that is, to be able to state and demonstrate that one particular temperature is twice, three times, or *n* times greater than another). Nevertheless, even simple "adjustment" presupposes the *concept* of temperature and its *articulation* with *other concepts*. For example, the concept of *expansion:* the operation of the experimental apparatus that constitutes a thermometer, as an instrument of adjustment, not of measurement, implies that a conceptual relation has been established between temperature and expansion.

10. The concept of "socially necessary labor-time" is only *posed* by Marx in volume one of *Capital* and is not fully developed until volume three: it is there we see that equal participation of the capital invested in the different branches of production (i.e., the equalization of profit rates) is the condition under which labor expenditures carried out in the different branches *are* socially necessary (that is, as long as the enlarged reproduction of capitalist relations of production is accomplished through the competition of capital in the different spheres of investment).

11. To say that the distribution of labor must be "regulated" by the social utility of this labor and its products is not to say that this social utility is to regulate this distribution by itself.

12. See V. V. Novozhilov, "Mesures des depenses (de production) et leurs resultats en économie socialiste" in *Rationalité et calcul économique en URSS*, ISEA (February 1964): 43–292. In this same volume, references will also be found to the works of V. S. Nemtchinov and L. V. Kantorovitch. The work of the latter author has been translated into French: *Calcul économique et utilisation des resources* (Dunod Editeur, 1963). This work is available in English as *The Best Use of Economic Resources* (Oxford, Eng.: Pergamon Press, 1965; Cambridge, Mass.: Harvard University Press, 1965).

13. It is this very problem of the effects of objective laws being "concealed" by "decisions" that E. Preobrazhensky raises in his work, *The New Economics* (London and New York: Oxford University Press, 1965).

14. The concept of "socialization of the productive forces" clearly has to be developed, since there exist several "types of socialization," notably a capitalist socialization and a socialist socialization of the productive forces. Nevertheless, even the capitalist socialization of the productive forces tends to reduce the role of direct labor in the production of use-value, and to increase that of "general labor," which can neither be "measured" under the same conditions as direct labor, nor subjected to the same type

of commodity relations as the latter. Marx indicates this in the following text:

"To the degree that labour-time—the mere quantity of labour—is posited by capital as the sole determinant, to that degree does direct labour and its quantity disappear [with the development of the productive forces—C.B.] as the determinant principle of production—of the creation of use-values—and is reduced both quantitatively, to a smaller proportion, and qualitatively as an, of course, indispensable but subordinate moment, compared to general scientific labour, technological application of natural sciences, and to the general productive force arising from social combination (*Gliederung*) in total production on the other side . . . Capital thus works towards its own dissolution as the form dominating production." (*Grundrisse*, p. 700)

15. The interdependence of the different sectors of the economy renders it impossible to consider the operation costs of one sector independently from the costs of other sectors, and also, therefore, from the repercussions of the activity of this same sector on the other sectors.

16. On this point, see the quotation from Marx in note 14, above.

17. Furthermore, this sum is itself difficult to calculate, since it is a question of forms of production that are complex and conjoined.

18. Of course, the fact that these "errors" are committed can satisfy the interests of determinate classes, and this is not without effect on the reproduction of these errors.

19. Part of what is simply enumerated here will be developed later on in the text. However, it will not be possible to undertake an analysis here of the influence exerted by the existence of a world capitalist market, one of the principal obstacles to a full development of socialist relations of production. This would require too long a treatment and would take us far from the problems that are central to this text. By way of indication, however, we can state that as long as a world capitalist market exists, *worldwide capitalist relations penetrate* the production process of existing transitional social formations; this produces a series of effects, including effects at the level of economic calculation.

Chapter 2

The "presence" of commodity categories

The "presence" of commodity categories in contemporary transitional social formations raises fundamental theoretical problems.[1] In effect, this "presence" cannot be explained either in voluntarist terms or on the basis of mistaken predictions.

The first "explanation" would consist in saying that value continues to be "attributed" to different products because of "governmental decision."

The second "explanation" would involve saying that Marx and Engels were "mistaken" when they "forecast" that the value-form must disappear in socialist society.

The first "explanation" does not explain anything, since the value-form has an *objective existence*. It manifests itself when the conditions of its appearance are given. This objective existence asserts itself independently of any "governmental decision," and even *against* such decisions.

Moreover, talk of "mistaken predictions" is beside the point since neither Marx nor Engels indulged in prediction. On the one hand, they *analyzed* the social conditions under which the value-form appears; on the other, they characterized socialist society as being a social formation in which definite relations of production are established such that the *conditions for the appearance* of the value-form are not given.

If the value-form and prices still exist in present-day transitional social formations, it is precisely because these formations are still not fully developed socialist formations.

Consequently, it is necessary to go beyond subjectivist explanations (in terms of "will" or "error"). To do this, we must first of all recall the *social conditions* that determine the appearance and development of the *value-form*. By doing this, we will be able to bring to light the conditions for the appearance of this form within actual, transitional social formations. At the same time, this will enable us to see better how and why a number of the social relations characteristic of these formations are not those of a developed socialist society. It is by defining the character of the social relations appropriate to both the transition and the requirements for the passage to socialism (requirements that can be understood all the better as a result of the analysis of the historical experience of forty years of transition) that the functions planning and economic and monetary calculation fulfill in transitional social formations can be determined.

1. *Value-form and the conditions of production*

If in the eyes of a certain ideology the presence of the value-form and its transformed forms within present-day "socialist economies" is only a "survival," it is because they represent determinate *social relations*. Consequently, these forms can only "appear" when these social relations exist.

This takes us back to the fundamental analyses of Marx and Engels, which clearly show that it is only *under particular social conditions* that products are transformed into commodities—that is, into "sensuous-supersensuous things," into things endowed concomitantly with "physical" qualities and a measurable "economic" quality—the capacity of being exchangeable in determinate proportions with other products.

It is this latter "property" (which "belongs" to things in as much as they are "commodities") that is termed their "value." The "value" of things and exchange are so indissolubly related that value, in as much as it is a "general property of things," cannot continue to exist when commodity production has been replaced by production intended not for exchange but for the satisfaction of social needs. It is this fundamental relation between value and commodity production that Engels explains in a letter to Kautsky on September 20, 1884.

In this letter, having criticized Rodbertus, who considered capital to be "eternal," Engels adds:

> You make the same mistake with *value*. [According to you—C.B.] current value is that of commodity production, but, following the abolition of commodity production, value would also be "changed," that is to say, *value in itself* would continue to exist, and only its form would be modified. But in fact, however, economic value is a category specific to commodity production, and *disappears* with the latter, as it likewise did not exist prior to commodity production. The relation of labour to the product, before as after commodity production, is no longer expressed under the *value*-form.[2]

This formulation takes us back to the analyses in *Capital*. Indeed, this is the very problem that Marx puts forward in the following two sentences, which introduce an analysis of the value-form. "We have now determined the substance and the magnitude of value. It remains for us to analyse the form of value."[3]

These two sentences bring to light what, on this point, radically differentiates Marx's analysis from that of classical political economy. The latter had analyzed value and the magnitude of value, and had discovered, at least in its essential aspects, what is at the same time both represented and hidden by the value-form (viz., labor and time of labor), but it had ignored a fundamental question: why do labor-time and the relation between the labor-times of producers not appear as such? Why are they represented under the value-form?

These questions are crucial, primarily because of the dissimulating function that is peculiar to the value-form. In effect, this form conceals the specific object of economic science and similarly hides the specificity of commodity economy.

(a) The dissimulation of the specific object of economic science

The value-form conceals the specificity of economic science. When the former is present, this presence seems to "indicate" quite adequately the field of political economy, with the result that everything that is "endowed" with value would enter into this field.

COMMENTS

When Bukharin committed the error, which was denounced by Lenin, of stating that socialism signified the "end of political economy," he did not go beyond this immediate representation peculiar to commodity production. Such a proposition effectively reverts to an identification of the *object* of political economy with the *value-form* and its developments, thereby either "forgetting" that the Marxist science of the economic level has as its object the analysis of the effects of the double articulation—productive forces/relations of production—or "thinking" that a form of production could exist that would contain no relations of production but only productive forces, and that it would, therefore, simply be a question of the "technical organization" of labor processes. Yet, production, in as much as it is a *social process*, can never be "reduced" to productive forces alone, as it always implies determinate relations of production, that is, the type of complex structure that is the very object of Marxist economic analysis.

The field of political economy and the phenomena that "occupy" it would thus be both immediately *given* and *observable*. Consequently, political economy would be a science that would have no need of a concept of its object. It could even be "founded" as a science in the very absence of this concept, since the latter would be a proper quality of "objects" of its field, which would be sufficient to "recognize" the latter. In other words, the *property* of these "objects" would be completely homogeneous, comparable, and *directly "measurable."*

Therefore, the presence of the value-form makes the necessity of the construction of the concept of political economy, as it were, disappear; political economy itself fails to examine this disappearance. It is this very characteristic of the problematic that Marx distinguishes when, speaking of the classics, he states: "They exclusively gave their attention to the quantitative aspect of the question." [4]

This remark is of the utmost importance for us, since, with regard to the economic relations (relations of production, circulation, and consumption) that give rise to the existence of the value-form, the *dissimulating effect* lasts as long as this very form continues to exist—as long as a problematic is not taken up that puts the latter resolutely *in question*. This likewise explains why a considerable number of economists in the "socialist" countries can consequently be much more preoccupied with the problem of the "measurement of value" than with the problems posed by the very existence of this form in contemporary transitional social formations.

COMMENTS

We know that Marx discovered the determination of value by abstract labor, that is, by labor in as much as it *reproduces* the social conditions of production, the *relations of production*. While the disappearance of commodity relations clearly cannot bring about the disappearance of reproduction of the relations of production that is carried out by abstract labor, it does necessarily modify the *form* in which this labor manifests itself. The latter is then no longer the *value-form*, and the *dissimulating effect* of the relations of production produced by this form is also different.

The empiricist-positivist definition of the object of political economy, an "object" reduced to a homogeneous space where everything "is measurable," [5] requires those who want to establish a theoretical foundation for such a political economy to refer to "a certain world outside its own plane which has the theoretical role of underlying its existence and founding it." [6]

This "world outside," on which non-Marxist economists hope to found the "given" object of their discipline, is, naturally (for those who accept the evidence of the "given" and, consequently, the form of the "autonomous subject" under which the agents of the social process of production are presented), the "world of needs" subjectively experienced by human beings. This is why the human subject of classical and neoclassical political economy is one "fallen prey to needs." Behind the empiricism of value as a given, a naive ideological anthropology is constructed, the first formulation of which is given in Hegel.[7]

Because this step of constituting the notion of *homo economicus* is taken, the *given* of political economy (as it is, in actual fact received) is *hidden behind an ideology* in whose name particular phenomena are declared to be "economic" in so far as they are the direct or mediated effects of the needs of human subjects.

Since the subject of economic anthropology is "eternal," needs are thought of as universal. Consequently, "economic laws" are endowed with the same universality, and the notions operative at the level of a particular economic *practice*, such as the notion of "optimum," will also possess this "universality."

We will see later on that a number of economists from the "socialist" countries, who have similarly devoted all their attention to "value as a quantity," have accepted the value-form as a given that poses no problems. This factual acceptance leads to the acceptance of "universal economic laws," even if this is not recognized in words.

These, then, are just some of the ideological effects produced by the dissimulating function of the value-form when this form is not subject to a critical analysis. If we are not to be victims of this dissimulation, it is quite inadequate to say, as Ricardo did, that "The substance [of exchange-value] . . . is labour." [8] Rather, it is essential to ask *what* is the character of the labor that is "represented" under this form, and *why* the latter is represented in this way.[9]

In posing these questions, we find that it is only labor inscribed in particular *social relations* that takes the value-form. Consequently, posing the question of value as a *form* requires the production of the concepts "social relation," and more particularly, "relation of production." It is in this way that the theoretical process, which permits the foundation of the space of the economy itself, is begun. This process also enables the concept of different *modes of production* to be produced, and, as a result, the substitution of a structured and complex space for the homogeneous space of non-Marxist political economy.

(b) *The dissimulation of the specificity of commodity economy and of the content of the value-form*

A second aspect of the dissimulating function fulfilled by the value-form is that it "represents" what it is by concealing the latter, and by concealing it in a contradiction. Consequently, when we say that twenty yards of linen = one coat, not only do the *contents* common to the two terms (the knowledge that they are the product of a particular social labor, and of a particular quantity of this labor) not appear (and are therefore hidden), but the exchange-value of the coat has no part in this relation (from which it is, therefore, absent) since this exchange-value is itself "represented" by its "opposite," that is, by a use-value (a coat).

The value-form is, therefore, the expression of an "identity of opposites." As Marx showed very precisely, this contradictory character of the value-form and of commodity production in general has its origin in the doubly contradictory character of the labor peculiar to commodity economy, that is, in the contradictory identity of "private labour that must at the same time be represented as social labour." [10] This mode of existence of the identity of opposites inherent in commodity economy is fully developed in the capitalist mode of production, the most advanced form of commodity production. [11]

The specific form in which the double character of labor is represented in commodity production is the result of the specific complexity of the relations in which labor and its products are involved. Thus, this form is the *effect of a particular complex structure*, whose elements are simultaneously related in several ways (hence the specific profundity of social space). Some of these relations conceal others; as a result, they seem to possess an "autonomy" and "properties" that they do not really have, hence the paradoxical character of a reality that is only an "appearance" [12] (a "phantasmagorical" [13] reality, according to Marx).

Such a reality must, therefore, be analyzed in order to discover, or rather to reconstruct, the *real movement* which cannot be observed in that reality. The knowledge of this movement must, therefore, be "produced" by science. Science alone can "see" it, while "appearance" continues to impose itself on immediate representation under the modality of commodity "fetishism."

By examining the composition of the double character of labor more closely and the complexity of the structure that is revealed by this character, we will see more adequately the nature of the social relations and the identity of opposites that is concealed by the value-form. This should enable us to understand both *why* this form is still present in social formations in transition between capitalism and socialism and the *function* that it can fulfill in these formations.

Firstly, let us recall that the commodity form of production (commodity relations) is not identical to the CMP since this form does not necessarily imply the *class relations* specific to the capitalist mode of production; it only implies the existence of independent "private" producers, who exchange commodities with each other. Thus, the commodity form of production exists within the feudal mode of production, as that of independent small producers ("simple commodity production"); and it can also exist, as we shall see, in the transitional form between capitalism and socialism. As for the CMP, it is characterized by the existence of the *wage-relation*, in as much as this relation subjects labor-power to the requirements for the increase of value. The CMP presupposes that workers have been *separated* from their means of production and that they can only put these to work under the aegis of capital (value functioning through its self-incrementation). The wage-relation itself, and the reproduction of this relation, implies the transformation of labor-power into a commodity, and, consequently, the penetration of commodity relations even into the processes of labor and production. Capitalist relations of production are those that link the bearers of labor-power (the working class) to those who "own" the means of production (the capitalist class). By their very nature, these are relations of exploitation—it is only because of this that capitalist and worker are bound together. These relations subject the immediate producers to capital, the latter always functioning as *social capital*, of which the *individual* capitalists are never more than *agents* or, as Marx said, *functionaries*.

The double character of labor peculiar to the commodity form of production results precisely from the fact that, while labor appears to be expended as *private* labor (the "concrete" labor of an "independent subject"), it is also *social labor* ("abstract" labor through which the social conditions of production are reproduced). Thus, as *commodities*, products are the result of social labor that is "represented" as private labor.

COMMENTS

The double interrelation of "private" labor/"concrete" labor *and* "social" labor/"abstract" labor suggests the possibility that the disappearance of the contradiction "private" labor/"social" labor also involves the disappearance of the contradiction "concrete" labor/"abstract" labor. This is one way of conceiving the disappearance of all relations of production and, consequently, of identifying the end of political economy with the disappearance of commodity relations.

As we have already noted, the disappearance of the contradiction private labor/social labor must involve a *transformation of the form of appearance* of the contradiction concrete labor/abstract labor, and, therefore, the formation of a space of representation other than the market. In the present state of economic theory and practice, it seems that it can be stated that this other "space" or representation is that of the "plan." In this space, the social process of production is represented under the form of "the organization of the productive forces," which constitutes a specific form of dissimulation of the relations of production. Although this point cannot be developed here, it is essential to add the following: it is clearly necessary to make a distinction between the plan as a *space of representation*, within which economic relations are inserted, and the plan as a unity of concrete objectives and obligations resulting from an effective *economic and political practice*.

Note that the commodity form *conceals* the relation between the two types of labor by *inverting* it, since, in this form, private labor is "represented" as social labor. Such an inversion also affects the "value" of labor-power, which appears as "value of labor." As Marx said, "This phenomenal form makes the real relation invisible, and even shows the direct opposite of this relation." [14] The *social relation* that underlies the double character of labor—social and private at one and the same time—is the relation between "independent" producers, who are dependent upon each other, not as the subjects but as the agents of a process of social production. The material basis of this process is formed by the *labor processes* based upon determinate means of production, which supply the *products* that serve as *"supports" for the connections between labor processes.*

The specific complexity of the structure, which we have mentioned earlier in the text, means that the relations among producers are "doubled" by the relations among *owners* of products. These relations conceal the former, because those who appear in exchanges do so not as *producers* but as *owners* of products. (This opposition clearly becomes most significant under capitalist production, in which the two forms are *separated* and play an inverted role: the capitalist *owners* of products appear under the form of *producers*, which they are not.) As far as the owners who participate in exchanges are concerned, their products are not use-values or exchange-values, and so the *concrete labor* that has provided these use-values must be at the same time *abstract labor*, labor that produces commodities.

Consequently, in commodity production, the relations that unite the participants in exchange also link objects to "independent/dependent" producers who intervene as owners and who only take part in exchanges to the extent of even ceasing to be the owners of the objects that enter into exchanges; it is this structure of relations which explains that:

The value-form and the value relation of the products of labour . . . has absolutely nothing to do with the physical nature of these products, and with the relations between things [*dinglich*] which are the result of that form. It is only a determinate social relation between men which here dreams up for them the phantasmagorical form of a relation between things themselves.[15]

This same complex structure, which explains the specificity of the identity of opposites, also manifests the expression of the value-form, in which an (absent) exchange-value is "represented" by a use-value. This form of "representation," which is also a form of inversion, is a property of a structure in which *social* labor is *private* labor. In effect, it is due to the complexity of the structure that the same element is simultaneously present in *two relations*, one of which conceals the other; in other words, the former relation can possess properties which are the inverse of the relation that it conceals, but this clearly does not prevent the two relations being real.

COMMENTS

If what we have said in previous "Comments" is correct, then the socialist mode of production must consequently also possess specific forms that conceal real relations, the place of these dissimulating forms being the "plan." If this is the case, then the specific complexity of the relations that the plan simultaneously reveals and conceals also requires a *theoretical analysis*. The absence, or inadequacy, of this analysis can be the source of a "fetishism of the plan."

This conclusion shows us the ideological character that the opposition "plan/market" can assume. When the plan is "thought" in the form of immediate representation, it effectively appears to be simultaneously both the *opposite* and the *same thing* as the market. This character of identity of opposites signals an *ideological coupling* and thus an opposition, which is at the same time both illusory and real.

Within this ideological coupling, the plan appears to fulfill the "same functions" as those of the market, but "under another form."

It is this ideological coupling that supports Pareto's and Barones' theses[16] on the identity of the effects of "perfect planning" and "perfect competition," theses that are found again, transformed, in the work of a number of economists in the "socialist countries." We will return to the function that the ideological coupling, "plan/market," fulfills later, but we should note here that it relates to a *specific difference that is not the one it claims to exhibit:* what is in question is not (and, moreover, cannot be) a difference in forms but a difference in functions. The latter is hidden by this ideological coupling, which ultimately plays an important role in the political struggles of the transitional period. Furthermore, the same dissimulation operates through the ideological use of the coupling, "monetary calculation/direct economic calculation." With regard to this, we will subsequently analyze the meaning of Soviet and Hungarian economists' use of this coupling, and, in particular, their use of the *duality theorem*[17] (in this, they follow the road opened up by a number of Western European economists[18]).

The preceding developments have not, of course, taken us far away from the two interconnected problems that are the principal ones facing us: those of the existence of market categories in social formations in transition between capitalism and socialism, and of the social relations concealed by these categories. On the contrary, it is on the basis of these comments that we can now make a number of observations on the *double existence* of commodities.

(c) The double existence of commodities

Commodities are objects that concomitantly "have a value" and are "socially useful."

In commodity forms of production, the *principal aspect* of products is that they are objects having a *value*. This is why, according to Marx's expression, wealth presents itself as an "immense accumulation of commodities." [19] Here their character as "socially useful" objects is only of interest because it enables them to be commodities, that is, to be precisely objects that "have a value."

In contrast to commodity forms of production, in the socialist mode of production,[20] products are no longer the result of "private labor" (in any sense of the word) and are thus no longer destined for *exchange.*[21] Consequently, they are no longer "bearers" of the contradiction of labor that is simultaneously "private" and "social." They are the result of *socialized labor.* Here, social wealth is no longer formed from an "immense accumulation of commodities," but from socially useful objects, that is, from objects produced for the satisfaction of "social needs."

In the analysis of a fully developed socialist society (in which not only *socialist relations of production* but also the *socialist mode of production* is dominant), the central place that the *analysis of value* occupied in commodity society must be filled by the analysis of what Marx called "real wealth," that is, of use-values and "socially useful effects."

COMMENTS

Perhaps it is useful here to recall that—in contrast to the wealth of societies in which the capitalist mode of production prevails—Marx, in using the term "real wealth" meant *use-values.* For example, in the *Critique of the Gotha Programme,* he said: "Labour is not the source of all wealth. Nature is just as much the source of use-values (and it is surely of such that material wealth exists) as labour, which itself is only the manifestation of a force of nature." [22] Marx's comment here is similar to the following passage from the *Grundrisse*:

> But to the degree that large industry develops, the creation of real wealth comes to depend less on labour time and on the amount of labour employed than on the power of the agencies set in motion during labour time, whose "powerful effectiveness" is itself in turn out of all proportion to the direct labour time spent on their production, but depends rather on the general state of science and on the progress of technology, or the application of this science to production. . . . Real wealth manifests itself, rather—and large industry reveals this—in the monstrous disproportion between the labour time applied, and its product.[23]

Several pages later, Marx makes this observation, which is directly concerned with the problem that we started with: "The measure of wealth is then not any longer, in any way, labour time, but rather disposable time." [24]

Such an analysis imposes new tasks, tasks which were uncalled for in the analysis of commodity production, since it requires the introduction of concepts whose pertinence would be challenged if it was simply a question of analyzing commodity production.

In particular, note that the relation between socially useful objects and the "social needs" they must satisfy calls for an analysis of this last term. This must be all the more rigorous since the concept of "need" is an ambiguous concept in so far as it does not have a precise social character. This is why the introduction of the concept of "human needs" leads to an ideological anthropology that obliterates the specific differences between modes of production and claims to found "universal economic laws," which are totally nonexistent.

In social formations in transition between capitalism and socialism, the existence of the value-form—and, consequently, of the corresponding relations of production, which is a point we will come back to in the next paragraph—is always the sign of a particular type of complexity of the economic structure, and of a particular mode of dissimulation and inversion. But, in addition to this, "social property" [25] in the means of production and planning—which is then the "scene" in which the unity of the labor processes is represented—leads to the appearance of a new form of "social" labor. This implies that the social process of production can have as its principal aim not the self-incrementation of value, but the increase in use-values. This is why, despite the fact that the value-form continues to exist in these social formations, social wealth is no longer reducible to an "accumulation of commodities," since it is also, and above all, the provision of use-values. The *double form* of "wealth" in transitional economies is thus directly related to the *double form* of "economic calculation": or, more correctly speaking, economic calculation and monetary calculation. We are thus brought back to the problem of the nature of the social relations that determine the existence of the value-form in transitional social formations.

2. Social formations in transition between capitalism and socialism, and the existence of the value-form

From the preceding discussion, we should draw two conclusions, both of which require the posing of a fundamental theoretical and practical question.

These two conclusions are as follows:

(1) If the value-form continues to exist in actual transitional social formations, *this is due to the persistence of determinate social relations that continue to assume the "phantasmagorical form of a relation between things."*

(2) Not only does the existence of this "phantasmagorical form" continue to "represent" relations between human beings as relations between things, but it also produces the form of inversion. As long as this form remains unanalyzed, it prevents the *real movement* of the relations between things from being understood. Furthermore, when this understanding is absent, the action of the political on the economic level is carried out in a very approximate manner, due as much to inadequate *knowledge* (of measurement and calculation) as to the instruments of action (adequate forms of organization, significant prices, etc.).

Clearly the question is the following: what are these "determinate social relations," the existence of which attests to the value-form's apparent "survival" of the elimination of private ownership of the means of production?

In general terms, an answer to this question is given in the very text of Marx cited above: "In general," says Marx, "objects of utility only become commodities because they are the products of different kinds of labour carried out independently of each other." [26]

Clearly, this general response must be made more concrete by specifying the *form* in which "the different kinds of labour carried out independently of each other" exist.

This question is of decisive importance, as much for a theoretical understanding of the very particular type of transitional social formations that we are concerned with (thus, with the specific characteristics of these social formations) as for an understanding of the role of the value-form and the characteristics presented by economic calculation in these social formations.

Therefore, we ought to dwell on this question at some length, first by recalling a number of the answers that have been given to it.

(a) A historical account of the answers given to the question of the existence of commodity categories in social formations in transition to socialism

If we examine this question by taking as a basis some of the theoretical responses that have attempted to answer it, we see that the content common to the greater part of these has, until now, been as follows. The value-form continues to exist because *several forms of ownership* of the means of production exist within transitional social formations: state property, the collective property of cooperatives, and, occasionally, "private" property. On the basis of this established fact, the existence of the value-form is explained by the fact that exchanges between the different owners of property, and thus the very acts of buying and selling, are brought about by this form. Or again, it is said that the value-form still exists because it is through buying and selling that the social character of the labor, carried out in the different units of production belonging to different property owners, asserts itself.

In substance, this is the answer given by Preobrazhensky in 1927, in his work *The New Economics*,[27] an answer that had already appeared in a previous work by the same author, *From NEP to Socialism*.[28]

This is the same reply that Stalin gave to this question twenty-five years later, in conditions profoundly modified by collectivization and the disappearance of private capitalism (since the latter still existed in the period of the NEP).

In *Economic Problems of Socialism in the USSR*, Stalin wrote:

Today, there are two basic forms of socialist production in our country: state, or publicly owned production, and production which cannot be said to be publicly owned.

The effect of this is that the state disposes only of the product of the state enterprises, while the product of the collective farms, being their property, is disposed of only by them. . . . At present, the collective farms will not recognize any other economic relation with the town except the commodity relation—exchange through purchase and sale. Because of this, commodity production and trade are as much a necessity with us today as they were, say, thirty years ago, when Lenin spoke of the necessity of developing trade to the utmost.

And Stalin adds: ". . . when instead of the two basic production sectors, the state sector and the collective farm sector, there will only be one all-embracing production sector, with the right to dispose of all the consumer goods produced in the country, commodity circulation, with its 'money economy,' will disappear, as being an unnecessary element in the national economy." [29]

From this particular formula (which invokes a "subjective" justification: the acceptance or nonacceptance by the collective farms of other economic relations), it would appear that the reply is that the existence of commodity categories is really the result of the existence of two forms of property.

The same reply is found in the *Handbook of Political Economy* published by the Academy of Sciences of the USSR, and it is still the one generally given today in the "socialist" countries. This reply is obviously not false, but it is *inadequate.*

It is correct, in that it clarifies what has been (and, in a certain number of cases, continues to be) one of the "legal bases" for the existence of commodity categories in transitional social formations.

Yet, the existence of a state sector alongside a cooperative or collective farm sector, as one of the bases for the existence of the value-form in social formations in transition from capitalism to socialism, ought not to conceal the existence of an *economic base*, which is the principal foundation. It is this that is of the utmost importance theoretically and historically since it exists throughout the entire transitional period between capitalism and socialism. The knowledge of this base is of decisive practical importance—to the extent that it gives rise to *contradictions* which require an adequate treatment.

Before examining this economic basis for the existence of commodity categories, we must briefly state why the legal explanation, which refers exclusively to the existence of several forms of ownership of the means of production, is unsatisfactory.

This is so for the following reason: the existence of different forms of property ownership of the means of production does, indeed, explain the maintenance of commodity relations between the "different proprietors": between the state and the collective farms, the state and consumers, the consumers and collective farms, and between the collective farms themselves. However, the existence of these forms does not explain the maintenance of commodity categories, and, therefore, of buying and selling *within the state sector itself.*

Indeed, why, within the state sector, have the commodity forms and relations not disappeared? Why do the means of production have *prices*, and why are they *paid for* with a *money* that plays the role of a *general equivalent?* Why, within the state sector, are products *bought* and *sold*, and why are they *not* freely *distributed* among the state-owned enterprises? Why, as a result, must the state give its own enterprises the monetary and financial means that enable them to purchase the means of production they need?

The existence of other sectors and other forms of property clearly does not suffice to explain this state of things.

COMMENTS

To say, as some Soviet economists do, that the payments taking place between enterprises are not made in money because they are carried out by means of bank transfers, is a verbal contrivance that removes neither the intervention of *payments* nor the fact that these take place in the same money (the ruble, for example) that circulates elsewhere; the only thing that is different is this money's form of existence.[30]

Before trying to formulate an answer, it is useful to recall that the questions have not always eluded those who have supported the position that the existence of the value-form in contemporary socialist economies is explained solely by the existence of several forms of property in the means of production. Yet, while they have tried to answer these questions, the problematic that they have accepted at the outset has prevented them from giving satisfactory answers.

This is the case, for example, with Stalin's answer given in the text cited above. Here, Stalin puts forward as a principle that, within the state sector, the means of production are not commodities since:

> They [means of production] are only allocated by the state to its enterprises. In the second place, when transferring means of production to any enterprise, their owner—the state—does not at all lose the ownership of them; on the contrary, it retains it fully. In the third place, directors of enterprises who receive means of production from the Soviet state, far from becoming their owners, are deemed to be the agents of the state in the utilisation of the means of production in accordance with the plans established by the state.

COMMENTS

Note that the description given, which is as much one of the process of enlarged reproduction and accumulation as of the functions that the different units of production fulfill in this process, takes place entirely in legal terms (in terms of "ownership" and "agents of the state"), implying that some sort of identification exists between the juridical-political *superstructure* and the economic *base*.

Hence, the conclusion: "It will be seen, then, that under our system, means of production can certainly not be classed in the category of commodities." [31]

But, having said this, Stalin then poses the following question, to which he gives answers that we will now examine.

> Why, in that case, do we speak of the value of means of production, their cost of production, their price, etc.?
>
> For two reasons:
>
> Firstly, this is needed for purposes of calculation and settlement, for determining whether enterprises are paying or running at a loss, for checking and controlling the enterprises. But that is only the formal aspect of the matter.

Secondly, it is needed in order, in the interests of our foreign trade, to conduct sales of means of production to foreign countries. Here, in the sphere of foreign trade, but *only in this sphere*, our means of production really are commodities, and really are sold.[32]

Let us examine these two answers. The first is clearly inadequate. Furthermore, Stalin recognizes this when he says that he is only approaching the question from the "formal aspect of the matter." In fact, this reply refers to the necessities of "calculation," to the "regulation of accounting," and to the evaluation of the "profitability" of enterprises, etc. But this precisely raises more questions than it solves. The real problem is to know *why* it is necessary to carry out calculations *in value*, and why, *within the state sector*, are the calculations that Engels talks about not carried out, that is, calculations both in labor-time and in the useful effects of different use-values. Consequently, Stalin's reply only raises, under another form, the problem that needs to be resolved.

Note also that this first reply is the same as that already given by Preobrazhensky to the same question. Indeed, he writes that, in the transactions between state trusts, "the category of price assumes . . . a purely formal character." [33]

The question, therefore, remains the same. Why is it necessary to make use of a category that has a "purely formal character," in preference to other procedures?

Or why, in transitional economies, and within the state sector, are *actual prices* and not social evaluations used in "accounting"? (By actual prices we mean prices that are actually *paid*, which consequently give rise to a monetary circulation.)

COMMENTS

If, as there is every reason to think, social accounting must occur even within a fully developed socialist economy (where products, not being commodities, do not have prices), this accounting will require social evaluations. These will have to express the results of measurements and economic calculations. The existence of a system of social evaluations (the nature of which will have to be defined) is something quite different from that of a system of actually paid prices, which itself reproduces a system of monetary costs leading particularly to the appearance of *wages* as an element of these costs.

Before trying to answer these questions, let us examine the second explanation for the existence of the value-form in the state sector.

This explanation refers to the problem of exports. As it is presented here, this explanation is similarly quite unsatisfactory as it does not enable us to understand why means of production that are *not intended for export* retain the outward appearance of commodities. Nevertheless, it does indirectly indicate a very important fact, namely that in actual transitional social formations, the structure of national production (and thus of the internal division of social labor) and the conditions of reproduction, are related to the system of world prices; consequently, *they are only partially freed from the domination of the law of value* as it functions on the world market. This situation implies specific forms of combination between capitalist relations of production on a world scale and the socialist relations of production in the process of development (or decline) within these social formations.[34]

Before going any further, we must recall several other conclusions that have been drawn from the answers given in the texts of Preobrazhensky and Stalin to the questions posed above.

These conclusions assert not only that the means of production circulating between state enterprises are not commodities but also that, in general, as we shall see, within the state sector they are "false commodity categories," in the sense that they have a new "content." Here again, it is useful to see how Stalin draws these conclusions from the preceding formulations:

> If the matter is approached from the formal angle, from the angle of the processes taking place on the surface of phenomena, one may arrive at the incorrect conclusion that the categories of capitalism retain their validity under our economy. If, however, the matter is approached from the standpoint of Marxist analysis, which strictly distinguishes between the substance of an economic process and its form, between the deep

processes of development and the surface phenomena, one comes to the only correct conclusion, namely that it is chiefly the form, the outward appearance, of the old categories of capitalism that have remained in our country, but that their essence has radically changed in adaptation to the requirements of the development of the socialist economy.[35]

What can we conclude from this set of propositions?

Later on, we shall see that the way in which the relation *content/form* is formulated here is unsatisfactory, and we shall also see why this is so. But, for the moment, we will leave this aside and develop the consequences of this problematization, which will enable us to focus better on the main questions.

We will say, therefore, that according to Stalin's formulation, the *content* of the commodity "form" has changed, due to the very fact that there is state (and proletarian state) property ownership of the means of production; and because of this, new *relations of production* have been established.

But unfortunately, the reference to this *changing of "content" leaves the problem of the "survival" of the value-form unresolved:* in effect, the real problem is to know exactly *why* the means of production that circulate between the state enterprises *have precisely the "form" of commodities, despite state ownership.*

Thus, the problem posed remains unresolved: what is the *specific content* of the value "form" and the commodity "form" that appear within the state sector?—that is, *what are the social relations that are hidden by these forms?* why hasn't the change in social relations led to the disappearance of the old form?—that is, why, in spite of this change, do products continue to appear as commodities that have a "value"?

In actual fact, the real problem is this: why do social relations of a capitalist type continue to appear, *independently of the will of human beings*, under a "phantasmagorical form," that is, as relations between things?

In other words, why does *commodity fetishism continue to exist* even within the state sector? What must be explained here is the *contradiction* between perceptible reality *(Wirklichkeit)* and statements concerning the "formal" character of commodity relations in the state sector.

It is all the more important to produce this explanation, since it is clearly very dangerous for the development of a socialist economy to rely on the idea that, because of the existence of state ownership of the means of production, the value and commodity forms would have no more than a "formal existence," that is, they would be "secondary forms."

Indeed, if this were the case, *it could be concluded that there is no objection to allowing the development of forms that have a radically new content.*

Moreover, this is precisely the sort of conclusion reached by those who support the fullest use of commodity forms in social formations in transition between capitalism and socialism. This is particularly the case with the Soviet economist Liberman, who, referring to "commodity forms that have a radically new content within the socialist economy," can conclude that the development of these forms poses no threat to the future development of the Soviet economy toward socialism.

Having arrived at this point, the problem that has to be resolved is as follows: seeing that commodity categories do *exist* within the state sector, what are the specific *social relations* that are *concealed* but also *revealed* by these forms?

This question will only have been answered satisfactorily if the answer *also* explains *why* these specific social relations *do not appear as such* but *effectively assume* "phantasmagorical forms."

Marx's analyses provide us with what we need to produce such an explanation. As we have seen, they show us that the *dissimulating* effect of social relations is an effect of a *particular mode of the complexity of the structure,* of a complexity characterized by the *superimposition of different relations between the very elements of this structure.* It is to this complexity that the *concept* of "form" refers. Consequently, it is impossible to arrive at a satisfactory solution if, as in the texts cited above, a nondialectical opposition between "form" and "content" is used.

This sort of ideological opposition assumes that the "forms" would be, as it were, "recipients," within which one could "place" various "contents." However, the Marxist concept of "form" cannot be treated in this way. In Marx's analysis, form is a relation, and, thus, the value-form is a *commodity relation.*

This relation, as it is "represented" in an ensemble of social relations, is termed form because, at one and the same time, it conceals and reveals another relation.

Consequently, the value-form is a *relation between products* whose mode of existence presents itself under the form of quantity. It is also a relation between labor (and thus between the agents of this labor)—not between any labor but rather between different kinds of labor that, while being carried out *independently* of each other, nonetheless *depend* on each other in as much as they are "moments" of a social process of production.

The existence of the value-form signals the presence of this double relation. This is why the propositions put forward above do not really constitute an answer to the questions posed. However, at the same time, they do indicate the path that can lead to a satisfactory reply, namely the knowledge of the existence of a *change* in the relations of production, a change connected with the existence of a proletarian state.

This change takes place when the state *uses* the means of production as *social* means of production, that is, when it *acts as the proprietor* of these means through the intermediary of the units of production—the places where these means are directly brought under control and put into operation.

This *action* by the proletarian state takes the form of the *plan* and the planned relations that are derived from this plan. While it permits the continued existence of a certain "independence" between the labor carried out in the different units of production, this action partly *modifies*—if it is adequate—*the modes of the interdependence of the different* types of labor that constitute the social process of production.

In other words, change of content in the above propositions alludes to a change in the modes of existence of the interdependence of labor. This change is made *possible* by the transformation of legal property relations, *but it is not confined to this.* It implies a determinate *action*, that is, a *social practice* through which *the state and its dependent political, economic, and administrative institutions really coordinate* a priori the activities of the different units of production. The more this coordination is extended and deepened, the more the nature of the relations between the units of production, and even the character of these units, is modified; the more the operational field of market relations (i.e., the value-form) is *restrained;* and the more indispensable new modalities of *economic calculation* become.

Of course, the degree of real coordination (and, therefore, the extent to which the economic plan is *adequate*) does not depend primarily upon "planning techniques," nor upon detailed and scrupulous "administrative operations," nor upon officially announced "intentions." It depends, rather, upon objective *political conditions*—on the effective participation of the masses in the formulation and operationalizing of plans; and it depends upon *scientific conditions* (the plan only really coordinates the activities of different units of production if it is based on a scientific analysis of economic and social reality, and if it satisfies the requirements for scientific experimentation). Moreover, the second condition can only be realized to the extent that the first is also realized; knowledge of economic reality and scientific experimentation on a social scale (all these are radically different from the manipulation of accounting magnitudes that a number of "plans" are reduced to) only develop with the participation of the masses.

The realization of these conditions corresponds precisely to the development of *socialist relations of production*, to the domination of producers over the means of production and the results of production. This domination is itself only possible within the limits fixed by the level of development of the productive forces.

COMMENTS

The "limits" that the level of the development of the productive forces assigns to the development of socialist relations of production are related to the *modalities* of coordination between the processes of production. These modalities are necessarily *different*, according to the level of development of the productive forces and the *nature* of this development. In effect, depending on the particular case, the coordination of the processes of production can take the form either of a *centralized plan* or of the *superimposition of plans* that *coordinate* these processes. Planning in the People's Republic of China corresponds more and more to this second form; it aims to ensure a socially controllable articulation over the processes of production. Indeed, it seems that it is this second form which, at least in the present state of the productive forces, best enables the producers to dominate the means and results of their production. With regard to the *nature* of the development of the productive forces, this is itself dominated by the dominant relations of production. These points will have to be taken up again later in the text.

To the extent that the conditions outlined above are unrealized, the modalities of *interdependence* specific to commodity production assert themselves, as does the ensemble of forms under which the corresponding relations appear.

Such, in brief outline, is the basis that it seems necessary to work on in order to understand the existence of the value-form and the "functioning" of prices and money in actual transitional social formations. The points that have just been made clearly need to be made more precise; we will try to do this with regard to some of them in the following pages. Naturally, this precision has for its point of departure the *displacement* of the problematic that we have just initiated.

In effect, this displacement requires that the existence of *commodity relations* (that is, commodity forms) be explained by the existence of a *particular system of productive forces and relations of production*. Therefore, it is essential to try to specify the characteristics of both of these during the transitional period.

Given that relations of production only act upon determinate productive forces, we will begin by examining the latter; however, what will be said on this subject must always be interpreted in terms of the system of productive forces only existing as an articulation within a system of relations of production which both *dominates* it and gives it its *form*.

(b) The commodity categories, as they appear in the state sector, and the system of productive forces

Here, the starting point is Marx's formulation, cited above, according to which "objects of utility only become commodities because they are the products of different kinds of labour that are carried out independently of each other." [36]

Reflecting on this formulation, we can see that it expresses the idea that the transformation of products into commodities does not originate directly in the fact that products are the result of different kinds of labor carried out by the "owners of private property" (or by workers under the instruction of these owners, who have previously purchased their labor-power), but in the fact that they are, very precisely, "the products of different kinds of labour carried out independently of each other."

This proposition thus indicates a particular mode of articulation of labor, a particular structure of the processes of production. This mode of articulation is described very precisely as corresponding to "different kinds of labour carried out independently of each other." The term "independence" clearly does not indicate a simple "deficiency": the absence of a "social will" that would have "restored" dependence to these different kinds of labor by "conceiving" of them as such. What is alluded to in this text is both the absence of an *objective dependency* between the different kinds of labor (which indicates that, *within certain limits, they can be performed independently of each other*) and the existence of relations between producers and units of production that exclude relations of cooperation organized on a social scale.

As we know, what precisely characterizes commodity forms of production is that the "independence" of the different kinds of labor, that is, of the processes of labor, conceals the reciprocal dependence of the laborers. It is precisely this dependence that lays down the limits to the relative independence of the production processes. These limits are imposed upon the "independent" producers through the *law of value*. This brutally imposes *ex post facto* the reciprocal dependence of labor and its activities. Its action is indicated by the term "regulatory role" of the law of value.

When the *socialization of the labor processes and the transformation of the relations of production* permit a preliminary adjustment of these activities, but without the objective independence (from now on more limited) of labor having entirely disappeared, the law of value loses its regulatory role to the extent that the producers succeed in coordinating their activities in advance, primarily by means of an economic plan.

This last proposition implies that the law of value only operates within a particular structure of productive forces and relations of production. The law of value is thus a *form* of the law of the distribution of social labor. It implies the domination of determinate relations of production over particular productive forces, that is, over productive forces characterized by a determinate structure of the labor processes.

Having arrived at this point, we must examine what constitutes the domination of the relations of production over the productive forces.

(c) Relations of production
and processes of production[37]

To begin with, we will develop a number of general propositions related to the subject outlined above, before "applying" these to transitional social formations. In these developments, some of the formulations put forward must be considered provisional, and therefore contingent upon eventual correction.

The content of the term "relation of production" must initially be specified. By this term, we mean a *system of positions assigned to the agents of production in relation to the principal means of production*. This system determines the *position* of immediate producers and, eventually, that of nonproducers. These positions are nothing other than the places where particular *functions* are carried out (the processes of the appropriation of nature, the coordination of these processes, the distribution of their results, etc.).

The action of the relations of production appears particularly in its *effects* on the *bearers* of the different *functions;* it can form these bearers into *classes.* The action of the relations of production on the *labor processes* gives them the form of a *process of production.*

This process of production not only ensures the production/reproduction of *products* but also that of the *system of positions* assigned to the *agents* of production. Consequently, the *process of production* is also a process of *reproduction of the relations of production.*

This reproduction implies a particular *distribution of social labor* (under a double form: distribution between necessary and surplus-labor, and distribution between the sectors of social activity), and a particular *distribution of products* and, therefore, a *circulation* of these products, constituting a *process of distribution.* It is because this distribution is the effect of relations of production that Marx can state that the relations of *distribution* are only the "reverse" of relations of *production.*[38] Thus, *circulation and distribution* are "moments" of the process of *production and reproduction.*

Each type of relation of production is defined by relations of possession/property, and the precise content of these terms is modified according to the way in which each combines with the other.

Generally, possession is established by the *ability to put the means of production into operation.* Depending on the structure of the *labor process,* this capacity can be individual or collective, and possession can be jointly held in a partial holding, or not. With regard to *property* (as an economic relation)—it is constituted by the *power to appropriate* the objects on which it acts for uses that are given, particularly the *means of production,* and the power to dispose of the products obtained with the help of these means of production. This power can assert itself as a power of coordination or direction of labor processes and as a power of appropriation of the products obtained from a given utilization. The *power* that property establishes can only be effective if it is articulated on the basis of possession, either the agents of property also being the agents of possession, or the agents of possession being subordinated to the agents of property.

As power, property implies the existence of *ideological relations;* furthermore, if there is a noncoincidence between property and possession or between possession and holding, there is a division of society into *classes;* this implies relations of economic domination / subordination, which, in order to be maintained and reproduced, must be doubled by relations of political domination / subordination, articulated in state power, and thus in *political relations.*

Ideological relations and state power ensure the reproduction of property (in ideological terms, "respect" for it)- by imposing norms that permit this very reproduction of property relations.

Property and possession are exercised through a series of *functions*— coordination, direction, and control of the labor processes, appropriation of the means of production for given uses, appropriation of products. These functions can be carried out by the property owners themselves (the "bearers" of property relations) or by their representatives (their agents). The social distribution of these functions and of the polar executive functions constitutes the *social division of labor.* Consequently, the latter is an *effect of the relations of production.* It is the same with the division of tasks constitutive of labor processes, or the *technical division of labor.* This is always *subordinated* to the social division of labor, which means that the modalities of the distribution of tasks are always socially determined.

This social determination concerns as much the modalities of specialization and professional qualification as the concrete distribution of tasks within the "units of production" (or "centers for the appropriation of nature") and the fixing of boundaries and forms of existence of these "units of production" themselves. Thus, the system of the *units of production* and their connection (or the *division of social production*) also constitutes an effect of the *relations of production on the labor processes.*

COMMENTS 1

The feudal "manor," the artisan's workshop, manufacture, the capitalist enterprise, etc. constitute specific forms of existence of the units of production. These forms are not directly determined by the nature of the productive forces. They are the effect of relations of production on the productive forces; in the same way, the dimensions of these units of production, their internal organization, and the modalities of the relations between them, are the result of the action of relations of production on the productive forces.

One of the effects of capitalist relations of production is that, through the accumulation and concentration of capital (which is also the concentration of finance capital), a *division* is established between the level at which the *capacity appears to put the existing means of production into operation* (the "administration" of capitalist factories) and the *power to put new means of production* to particular use (e.g., the investments made by joint stock companies, or by a financial group in a determinate factory, the power to create new units of production or to suppress existing ones, to merge them together, etc.). This power (held, for example, by an administrative council) is itself distinct from the shareholder's legal property, although it can be dependent on the latter, at least within certain limits.

The reproduction of the technical division of labor and the social division of labor requires not only the reproduction of the material conditions of labor but also the reproduction of the *bearers* of these *functions* and *tasks*, and consequently the *preparation* of specialized agents and the *selection* of these agents *to conform to the requirements of the social conditions of production.*

The social (ideological) institutions that assume these reproductive functions (family, schools, university, etc.) also assume, simultaneously, the reproduction of the conditions of the social and technical divisions of labor, the first being dominant here over the second. The fact that certain ideological institutions reproduce *specific social conditions* explains how the functioning of such institutions in transitional social formations can, if they are not radically transformed, enter into contradiction with the initial transformation of the relations of production.

COMMENTS 2

A number of complementary remarks must be made here:

(1) At the analytical level, it is necessary to distinguish between the *relations of production*, that is, the system of positions assigned to the agents of production in relation to the principal means of production (a system which constitutes a fundamental *structure*) and the *social relations of production*. The latter are the effects of this fundamental structure. These effects concern the agents themselves (the division into classes, the social division of labor, the technical division of labor), as much as the forms of the labor process into which they enter, and the modalities of articulation of these processes (thus, the forms of the units of production, the latter's internal "organization," the relations between them, and, consequently, the division of social production).

(2) These social relations of production are "lived" by the different categories of agents under the modality of the representation of their "role" and of that of other categories of agents; this representation means that the social relations of reproduction are *doubled by ideological relations*. When these ideological relations are *in correspondence* with the social relations of production, they ensure the *identification* of the different categories of agents with their "role," and they guarantee, at their own level, the reproduction of the social relations of production. This reproduction is thus dependent on the dominant ideological relations (those that form the ideology of the dominant class and consolidate the dominant relations of production).

Thus, property as "power" over the means of production is also an ideological relation; it functions as power in as much as it is "recognized" as such, that is, as long as it is not brought into question by an ideological class struggle.

This process of class struggle is rooted in the objective contradictions between the interests of the different social classes, but it has its own dynamic. One of the factors of this dynamic is constituted by the "dislocation" between the "roles" for which the ideological institutions prepare the agents, and the "functions" that they will actually be able to assume. This dislocation is related to the specific rhythms through which the reproduction of the different social relations is achieved.

The "correspondence" of ideological relations and social relations of production indicates the capacity of the ideological relations to contribute, at their own level, to the reproduction of the social relations. This capacity implies that the ideological relations "represent" social relations of production by concealing them, at least in social formations that are divided into classes. The dislocation between roles and functions determines a noncorrespondence between the two categories of social relations (of production and of ideology).

(3) In societies divided by classes, ideological domination is not sufficient to ensure the power of the dominant class, and the relations of production must also, therefore, be doubled by *political relations* that are concretized by putting institutions and *means of repression* into operation; together, these constitute the state apparatus, which is objectively at the service of the dominant class. The political relations are themselves doubled by ideological relations that (as long as they are dominant) consolidate political power, by giving it the appearance of natural necessity, legitimacy, or popular sovereignty.

(4) The ensemble of social relations of production, of political and ideological relations, forms a complex structure, the elements of which are reciprocally "causes" and "effects" of each other or, more rigorously, "are supported by one another," to use Marx's expression cited above. It is the "support" that the different relations provide that enables us to understand how the existence of some of these elements, rooted in practices and concrete relations (organization of the units of production, forms of political power, ideological institutions) tends to reproduce the general unity of the structure.

When the coherence of certain types of social relations (their level of correspondence) is such that they *dominate* the ensemble of other social relations, and their own enlarged reproduction entails the disappearance or dissolution of other types of social relations, we can say that a *dominant mode of production* exists. If this is not the case—in particular, if there is a *revolutionary rupture* in the domination of particular social relations without the possibility of this rupture being followed by such a weakening of the social conditions characteristic of another mode of production that their disappearance can be assured— then we are in a *transitional period.* It is precisely the characteristics of such a period that require a specific intervention of political power in order that new social relations come to be increasingly dominant.

If property as a relation of production is constituted by a *determinate power* (thereby also implying an ideological relation), then the *exercise of this power is necessarily articulated in the state* and in the law. Consequently, property is likewise a *legal relation.*

Because property is the unity of a *plurality of relations* there can be specific dislocations between the relations of this plurality, dislocations that are specific to property itself. Thus, effective power can be exercised by agents other than those legally invested with this power: for example, within the social division of labor, the "representatives" of (legal) property owners can have such an autonomy in relation to the latter that the owners themselves are increasingly deprived of all real power. Such dislocations, which upset the conditions of reproduction of the relations of production, are always an effect of the class struggle; their development can either be encouraged or restrained by the structure of the production processes; in turn, the development of such dislocations can modify the social and technical divisions of labor.

COMMENTS

The plurality of relations constituting property must clearly not be confused with the plurality of concrete powers that make up a particular form of property. As we know, these constitutive powers correspond to the different possible uses of objects on which private property rests, and, consequently, on the different possible uses of the "products" obtained with the aid of these objects. This plurality of powers can itself be divided between the different categories of "bearers" or "agents."

On the basis of these formulations we will focus our analyses more particularly on private property as a relation of production. This will serve as the point of departure for "applying" these formulations to transitional social formations.

(d) Private property as a relation of production

Private property, in the sense of a *relation of production* (or an economic relation) corresponds to the power of a category of agents to allocate particular means of production for a given use, and to dispose of the products obtained from this utilization. If the power of property owners over the means of production takes the form of *separation* between a multiplicity of individual property owners of separate means of production, property is said to be "individual"; if this power takes the form of the *unity of a plurality of property owners* (separated from nonproperty owners), property is called "collective"; if the unity extends to the entire property owning class in a social formation, property is said to be "social."

COMMENTS

In the preceding statements, the terms "individual," "collective," and "social" indicate the *form* in which property is represented, that is, the nature of the *relations between property owners*. These terms are not concerned with the *content* of property (the fundamental relation that constitutes it) that remains *private* as long as property is that of a particular class (which has the power to utilize the means of production and the products obtained by this utilization). If it ceases to be the property of a particular class and becomes the property of the aggregate of producers, then *social appropriation* occurs. During the transitional period, when the producers are the owners of the means of production through the intermediary of the state or a collective institution, then there is social or collective property.

If the *individual private* property owner has the capacity to bring means of production into operation by him/herself, and if he/she does so, then we are faced with the combination, individual possession/individual ownership, and thus with the fusion of possession and property under the form of noncapitalist individual property. If this property is also legal ownership, then it corresponds to the *legal form of private property*.

Noncapitalist individual property presupposes not only a certain amount of power (a particular relation of production) but also a *structure of the labor processes* such that each property owner can effectively bring the means of production into operation by him/herself. Consequently, this property implies *a parceling out of the social process of production* among the centers for the appropriation of nature, these being owned by different industrial proprietors. Such a structure, which is that of simple commodity production, involves the transformation of products into *commodities*, and, therefore, circulation under the form of commodity exchange.

If, by being put into operation by wage laborers, the means of production (which belong to "private owners") are used in a process in which value undergoes a self-increment—this thereby presupposes the existence of a class of "free laborers" (i.e., a proletariat)—private property takes the form of *capitalist property*, and the owners of "private property" are then *capitalists*, bearers of the relation of capital exploitation/wage labor. Such a structure, which is that of the capitalist mode of production, implies that labor-power can be transformed into a commodity; this reproduction implies the development of processes of collective labor that are based on the use of *means of social production*. Such means of production can only be set in motion by collective labor. The capitalists, or their representatives, intervene in this collective labor as directors of the labor processes. Thus, the capitalists (or their representatives) possess the ability to put the means of production into operation; consequently, capitalist property implies the *nonpossession of the laborers*.

Once capitalist production is established on a social scale, the requirements for the reproduction of its material and social conditions are such that each *individual capital* can only function as a part of *social capital;* this is why even the capitalist can only function as *agent of this capital.*

Marx discovered the series of *contradictions generated by private ownership of the means of social production* and the obstacles that private property puts in the way of the development of the productive forces. These obstacles are formed, fundamentally, by private property as *legal relation.* At this juridical level, a number of the obstacles (notably those that arise from the size of each individual capital and the dimensions necessary for operating large-scale means of social production) are eliminated by the different legal forms of "capitalist social property," such as joint stock companies or capitalist state property. However, these *legal forms* of "social property" (even that of the state) do not alter the *private character of capitalist property* (the latter is then "social" capitalist property, in opposition to "individual" capitalist property).

This private character results precisely from the fact that this property belongs to a *class* that lives on the exploitation of another class and *deprives* the latter of *property* and *possession* of the means of production.

In addition, the development of legal "social" forms of capitalist property involves the dissociation of *agents* of property from agents of possession, since ability to put the means of production into operation is situated at the level of the various "enterprises," which can belong to the same capitalist. When this is the case, the directors of these enterprises are also the "functionaries" of capital; as for the *circulation of products*—between the different enterprises (even if they belong to a single capitalist, to a group of capitalists, or to the state)—it is a *commodity circulation;* consequently, products not only assume the value-form (which is the case in every unit of capitalist production that is a "unit for the incrementation in the value of capital"), but they manifest their *exchange-value* in concrete terms.

These points should obviously be developed further. On the one hand, the concept of "enterprise" should be made more specific and will be attempted later in the text; on the other hand, the content of the concepts, "property," "possession," and "holding" should be specified. In effect, these concepts indicate specific objects that allow variations related to the very modes of combination of these relations. Thus, we could clarify the different forms of dislocation between property and possession in the economic and in the legal sense, and the *contradictions* that can arise from these dislocations with regard to their *effects* on *class relations* (on the class struggle) and on the development of the productive forces. But this is not the object of this text. In effect, the preceding comments are essentially intended to contribute to the analysis of social formations in transition between capitalism and socialism. Thus, our objective is only to show how certain concepts can be put to work in the analysis of labor processes, relations of production, and legal relations. What has been said in the course of the previous pages will, therefore, now be applied to transitional social formations; this will be the object of the second part of this study.

Notes

1. Here, I am returning to some of the analyses I put forward previously (notably in *La Transition vers l'économie socialiste*), but I am drawing conclusions from them that are partly new.

2. See, Karl Marx–Friedrich Engels, *Briefe an Bebel, W. Liebknecht, K. Kautsky, und Andere,* I (Moscow: Marx-Engels Institute), pp. 355–58, letter to Kautsky, 20 September 1884. This letter is contained in Karl Marx and Friedrich Engels, *Selected Correspondence* (Moscow: Progress Publishers, 1955). This passage in the letter has not been translated in *Lettres sur "Le Capital"* (Paris: Editions Sociales, 1964), p. 344. Nor is it translated in the English edition of *Selected Correspondence*, where the letter appears on p. 378.

3. *Le Capital*, 1:62; *Capital*, 1:47.

4. *Le Capital*, 1:83; *Capital*, 1:49.

5. On this point, see Althusser, *Reading Capital*, part 2, chapter 7.

6. Althusser, *Reading Capital*, p. 161.

7. Althusser is absolutely correct when he notes that "Hegel provided the philosophical concept of the *unity* of this 'naive' anthropology with economic phenomena in his famous expression, 'the sphere of needs.'" (Ibid., p. 162)

8. Karl Marx, *Theories of Surplus-Value* (Moscow: Progress Publishers, 1968), 2:395.

9. On this point, see Marx's letter to Engels, dated 8 January 1868; also, J. Rancière, "Le Concept de critique et la critique de l'économie politique," in *Lire le Capital*, 1:129 (part of Rancière's text has been translated in *Theoretical Practice*, nos. 1, 2, 6).

10. *Le Capital*, 1:122; *Capital*, 1:114.

11. On this point, see the analysis of J. Rancière, in *Lire le Capital*, 1:127–33, 151–54.

12. *This appearance*, of course, *forms a part of reality;* it is an "appearance" because it appears directly, and because it seems to exhaust the real, even though it is only immediately "given."

13. See *Das Kapital*, 1:78. The term used by Marx in German is *phantasmagoriche*. It seems to me to be more correct to render this term as "phantasmagorical," than as "fantastic" or "phantomatic," as it has been translated respectively by Roy (Paris: Editions Sociales, 1:85) and by Rancière, in the text cited above (p. 134).

14. *Le Capital*, 2:211; *Capital*, 1:540. On this point, see also J. Rancière, in *Lire le Capital*, 1:154n.

15. *Le Capital*, 1:85. (Translation partly revised, following *Das Kapital*, 1:78.—Trans.)

16. In particular, see E. Barone, "Le Ministère de la production dans un état collectiviste," in *L'économie dirigée dans un régime collectiviste* (Paris: Libraire Médicis, 1939), p. 245n.

17. Notably Debreu and Allais in France, and Arrow and Koopmans in the United States.

18. In fact, it is a question of a particular "economic" interpretation of "Lagrange's multipliers." This problem cannot be developed here; it will have to be taken up again later on, in order to clarify the *limits* within which Lagrange's multipliers can, eventually, help in resolving particular planning problems.

19. As Marx stated in the first sentence of *Capital*.

20. The concept of "socialist mode of production" refers to a theoretical object, distinguished by the *domination of socialist relations of production over the productive forces*. It must not be confused with the concept of "form of transition to socialism," nor with that of "social formations in transition from capitalism to socialism" (this designates concrete objects).

21. This does not mean to say that the products do not have to *circulate* between the different units of production, and between these units and the units of consumption.

22. Karl Marx and Friedrich Engels, *Selected Works* (New York: International Publishers, 1968; London: Lawrence and Wishart, 1968), p. 315.
23. Marx, *Grundrisse*, pp. 704–05.
24. Ibid., p. 708.
25. By its very terms, the expression "social property" is clearly contradictory, but it does *indicate* a contradictory reality; the property of the state (as an organ of state power, which is *separated* from the producers, even if it is controlled by them) is property that the state takes hold of "in the name of society," according to Engels' formulation. This contradiction is specific to the *transition:* the ending of the transition must lead to the disappearance of the *state* and of "property," which then gives way to *social appropriation* by the community of producers.
26. *Le Capital*, 1:85; *Capital*, 1:72–73.
27. Preobrazhensky's book remains an important point of departure for all work on the problems that we are preoccupied with, despite criticisms that can be made of some of the conceptions that are defended in it, notably the concept of "primitive socialist accumulation."
28. A French translation of this book has been published by C.N.R.S. (Paris: 1966).
29. Josef Stalin, *Economic Problems of Socialism in the USSR* (Peking: Foreign Languages Press, 1972), pp. 15–16. (This translation is a reprint of the text given in the English pamphlet, published in Moscow in 1952, with "changes made according to other English translations of the pamphlet." This translation differs in some respects from the 1952 French translation, published by the PCF, which Bettelheim uses. Notably, *droit de propriété* is simply rendered as "ownership" on p. 127 of the Chinese version, and *les fondes de pouvoir de l'Etat* is rendered as "the agents of the state."—Trans.)
30. In the attempts made to distinguish between "real" money (bank notes) and "scriptural circulation," see M. Lavigne, "Planification et politique monetaire dans l'économie soviétique," *Annuaire de l'URSS* (Paris: Editions du C.N.R.S., 1969), p. 349n.
31. Stalin, *Economic Problems*, p. 53.
32. Ibid., pp. 53–54.
33. Preobrazhensky, *New Economics*.
34. On the question of capitalist relations of production on a world scale, see A. Emmanuel, *Unequal Exchange* (New York: Monthly Review Press, 1972; London: New Left Books, 1972), and the debate that I opened in this book on Emmanuel's theses.

35. Stalin, *Economic Problems*, pp. 54–55.
36. *Le Capital*, 1:85; *Capital*, 1:72–73.
37. An important part of the following formulations was suggested to me by Yves Duroux.
38. *Le Capital*, 8:252–58; *Capital*, 3:877–84.

Part II

State property, enterprise, and planning

Chapter 1

State property in social formations in transition between capitalism and socialism

The break with the domination of the capitalist mode of production, with the dominance of capitalist relations of production or other relations of production corresponding to private property in the means of production (such as the break that has taken place historically up until now in contemporary transitional social formations), has occurred first at the *political level*. It is concerned with the class character of state power, that is, with the nature of the class in power. It is identified with the transfer of power into the hands of the proletariat. This transfer of power is itself the result of a transformation in the relation of social forces, a transformation that follows from economic, ideological, and political struggles which have broken the domination of *some* of the political, economic, and ideological *relations* that were previously dominant. It is in this way that the transitional period between capitalism and socialism opens a period traditionally indicated by the expression, "period of the dictatorship of the proletariat."

Generally, what characterizes this transitional period is a particular form of "noncorrespondence" between the various social relations and within the different levels of social formation, particularly at the economic level; we will be primarily (but not exclusively) concerned with this noncorrespondence in the course of the following pages.

At the economic level, one of the transformations that introduces the transitional period is the *nationalization* of the principal enterprises, and, therefore, of the principal means of production, which thereby become *state property*. This transformation, as Lenin stressed,[1] is obviously concerned with property in its *legal form*. It is not identical to the "setting up" of a *power* and a *"social capacity"* for setting the means of production in motion and for disposing of products. Consequently, it is a long way from constituting a "socialization."

COMMENTS

The radical difference between (legal) nationalization and socialization is particularly clear in the case of agricultural land in the Soviet Union. As is well known, the land was nationalized in 1917. Yet, up until collectivization, the greater part of agricultural land continued to be used as before (although, of course, by different "users"). During the NEP, agricultural land continued (in fact) to be "bought" and "sold," and it began again to be concentrated in the hands of rich peasants. Even after collectivization, nationalization only gave the state very limited powers over the utilization of agricultural land, and what powers were obtained were done so through the actual transformation of relations of production.

Furthermore, as the *Critique of the Gotha Programme* points out, the very form of "nationalization" and of "state property" is still inscribed in the framework of what Marx calls "bourgeois law," which exists throughout the whole of the transitional phase. This "presence" itself is not an isolated legacy, since it "corresponds" to a part of capitalist social relations that has not yet been eliminated, and which will only be able to disappear when these relations themselves disappear. Now, the point here is that *a number of these relations are manifest precisely* through the existence of *commodity categories, the value-form, and monetary calculation*.

From what has been said previously, we can put forward the following proposition: the existence of the value-form in contemporary transitional social formations has its foundation in a particular structure of the field: relations of production/productive forces. This structure has as its effect that different processes of production can only be controlled *separately* within different units of production.

The units of production, or the "groupings" or "unions" of units of production that exert this control over these separate processes, that is, which have the ability to effectively control determinate processes of appropriation of nature (real appropriation) are, likewise, *the possessors of the means of production* they put into operation.

In the majority of the "socialist countries," possession of the means of production reverts to the "enterprises" (this is a generic term that is used particularly in the Soviet Union). When this possession is consolidated by corresponding legal relations, the enterprise is established as a "legal subject": it disposes of fixed and circulating capital, it buys and sells products, borrows from the banking system, disposes of liquid capital, etc. Consequently, this possession tends to assume the legal aspects of property. However, *as long as the state effectively exercises a proprietary power* over the enterprises, the actions they perform are legal to the extent that they are in sole possession of the means of production, products, and liquid capital that they have at their disposal, so that the legal actions they execute are legal through the authority of state ownership. For example, when a product is sold, the sum received by the enterprise in return for this sale enters into the *possession* of the enterprise and becomes state *property*.

One of the problems raised by this is as follows: beyond the appearance of legal subjects, *who* (that is to say, *what category of agents*) *is effectively in possession of the means of production,* of the fixed and circulating capital that can actually be disposed of? In the case of the Soviet Union, and of its state sector, which we will take as an example here, these agents are not the workers but the managers of the enterprises, and the directors of these enterprises nominated by the state, by governmental authorities.

Consequently, it is the managers of the enterprises who—within *the limits imposed by state property* as a relation of *production*—have the *effective power to dispose of* the means of production and products obtained through the operation of these means by the workers.

Concretely, the *plurality* of these capacities of disposition, each "rooted" in a determinate enterprise, is one of the objective bases for *commodity exchanges* between units of production.

Thus, the existence of state property "above" the possession of the means of production imposes limits on the enterprises' possession. It is because of these limits that possession, and the legally recognized "rights" that reinforce it, are not transformed into property pure and simple—on the condition that state property is an economic reality and not a simple legal fiction. This is the case: on the one hand, when state property effectively enables the governmental authorities to "reappropriate" all or part of what each enterprise possesses; on the other hand, when the state effectively *dominates* the use that the enterprises make of their means of production and products.

Such a domination can be more or less rigorous, depending on the *politics* followed in this domain by government authorities (and thus in the last instance on the effects of the class struggle operating in a field that has a structure determined by a given combination of productive forces and relations of production). In particular, this politics is expressed through the greater or lesser *degree of autonomy* accorded to the enterprises.

In actual fact, then, the "limitations" imposed on the "autonomy" of the enterprises are the manifestation of the *state's power to dispose of products and appropriate the means of production*. Thus, what appears negatively as a "limitation" on the enterprises is, positively, the effect of specific *relations of production*, of *property relations* (in the economic sense), which can be *socialist relations* to the extent that they really ensure the *domination of workers* over the conditions of production and reproduction, and, therefore, over the means and results of their labor.

COMMENTS

The above proposition implies:

(a) That the state's powers of disposition and appropriation over the means of production and products only constitutes an effect of socialist relations of production *in so far as* these powers really ensure the domination of the workers over the conditions of production and reproduction (that is, if they ensure a domination in a way that is effective and not simply formal, and therefore illusory).

(b) That these state powers are only one of the possible forms of existence of such domination, and certainly not the most developed form, since state property—even that of a workers' state—still corresponds to a *separation* of the workers from their means of production, and thus to a relation that Marx characterized as dependent upon "bourgeois law."

It can be argued that when the property of the people's communes is inserted into economic and political relations, thereby making it an organic part of a social formation which is also dominated by the power of the workers, then this constitutes a more advanced form of existence of socialist relations of production than state property "pure and simple."

What radically distinguishes the people's commune from a cooperative is that it is not only an economic unit, but also a *political unit,* a unit within which social and political requirements have priority over economic requirements. Furthermore, because of this dominance of political requirements, it has been possible, in the Soviet Union, to characterize the state enterprise as a "superior form of socialist property," *in comparison to* the kolkhoz (which forms a *collective enterprise*).

If what has been said with regard to the people's communes is correct, and if the *practice of economic and social calculation* in the Chinese people's communes corresponds to the nature of these units of production, to the extent that they are not solely units of production, then the concrete analysis of this practice must provide us with valuable lessons about the conditions for the development of such an SEC.

Reciprocally, the existence of the enterprise (in a rigorous sense of the term, a point that we will come back to later) appears negatively as a "limitation" on the state's power—and, beyond this, of the workers' power—of disposition and appropriation, and, positively, as an effect of specific relations of production, that is, capitalist relations of production. Hence the capitalist character of the enterprises' "self-administration." The "self-administrating" *enterprise* is inserted into the capitalist relations of production that it reproduces. In the absence of socialist planning, the enterprise (whether it is in charge of its own administration or not) is *dominated* by capitalist relations of production, and it can only operate with the aim of increasing the value of its capital. Of course, in a determinate concrete situation, forms of workers' self-administration can have beneficial effects for the workers, but these effects are only temporary.

This point will be developed later, but we can put it forward here in the following terms:

The enterprise (in the strict sense of the term) is a *capitalist apparatus;* it is one of the places where capitalist social relations are articulated, and within which these relations reproduce themselves. This is the case, as we shall see, even if these relations are dominated by relations of a different kind, which intervene from the political level. Only a "revolutionization" of these units of production, which have the form of "enterprises," can put an end to the existence of this capitalist apparatus and replace it with a new apparatus, in which socialist social relations are articulated and reproduced. Clearly, such a revolutionization cannot be "decreed," but can only be the result of a complex struggle, during which the specific traits of a new type of unit of production will be able to make their appearance. In effect, these traits must correspond to *objective requirements,* and these can only be brought to light through *practice.* They cannot be "imagined," since any attempt to resort to the "imagination" would be the best way to do no more than "rediscover" forms of organization that correspond to the old social relations.

COMMENTS

To say that the specific traits of the units of production that result from the "revolutionization" of enterprises (and which make them socialist units of production) must correspond to objective requirements is also to recognize that this "revolutionization" must inevitably be accomplished under different conditions, depending on the local structure of the field, relations of production/productive forces, within which the process of "revolutionization" develops. Thus, in China, the "revolutionization" of the cooperatives, and the subsequent transition to people's communes, took place under totally different conditions from the "revolutionization" of individual state enterprises that was begun during the course of the Cultural Revolution.

The capitalist character of the "enterprise" (which, primarily in industry, is the concrete "unit of production" on which, as a general rule, state property exerts its effects in transitional social formations) is due to the fact that its structure assumes the form of a *double separation: the separation of workers from their means of production* (which has, as its counterpart, the possession of these means by the enterprises, that is, in fact, by their managers), and the *separation of the enterprises from each other.* This double separation forms the central characteristic of the capitalist mode of production, and it serves as a support for the totality of contradictions of this mode of production, to the extent that this mode opposes the "private" character of property or possession to the social character of the productive forces. State capitalism and national-izations only provide the formal means for partially "overcoming" these contradictions, that is, in fact, *the means by which their effects can be displaced.*

As such means, state capitalism and nationalizations—even those put into operation by a workers' state—still do nothing more than displace the effects of the contradictions that result from the "private" character of the possession of the social means of production. If the change in the class character of political domination *opens the way* to the elimination of these contradictions, it is because it *opens the way to the elimination of the enterprise,* initially by "limiting" its autonomy, and then by making possible its "revolutionization."

1. The *"enterprise"* and the character of the double separation

The character of the double separation that is assumed by the structure of the "enterprise" is concerned with the totality of the relations peculiar to this apparatus.

In the first place—and this is the fundamental point—the character of the double separation is an effect of the *relations of production themselves,* and, therefore, an effect of the conditions in which *the combination of labor-power and means of production takes place* (under the domination of the relations of production). Within the enterprises, this combination is carried out under the *direction* of their managers, after the *labor-power necessary for the labor processes that are carried out in each enterprise* has been *purchased.* Thus, labor-power and means of production intervene in the process of production under the *value-form,* and the labor process is duplicated as a *process in which the value of the means of production undergoes a self-increment.* This process is one in which the value-form is produced and reproduced through abstract labor.

The character of the double separation that is assumed by the functioning of the enterprises is clearly related to the "degree of development of the social character of labor." However, this must not be "thought" of as the simple equivalent of the "level of development of the productive forces." In effect, it is not simply a question of a *level* of development, but also of the characteristics of the productive forces. These characteristics are themselves determined by the *nature of the relations of production within which the productive forces have developed historically.* Thus, machine industry and the industrial enterprise are "products" of the *capitalist* development of the productive forces, that is, of the development of these forces under the domination of capitalist relations of production. The characteristics of the productive forces that are "inherited" by social formations in transition between capitalism and socialism have in turn to be profoundly transformed. At the economic level, the period of transition toward socialism is the period during which socialist relations of production *transform* the character of the productive forces.

COMMENTS

The above propositions imply that the relations of production exert a dominating effect on the characteristics of the means of labor (and, therefore, on the conditions of articulation of the labor processes). In effect, history shows that changes in the material conditions of labor (the productive forces) are realized after changes in the social conditions of production (in the relations of production).

It is in this way that the wooden plough, the harness, and the stirrup are products of feudal relations, that is, of serfdom and the mode of military struggle corresponding to it. Similarly, machine industry is developed within capitalist relations of production.

The productive forces that develop within given relations of production do not "produce" new relations of production; if they "shatter" the relations within which they are developed, it is through economic and, ultimately, social contradictions, which involve the *dissolution* of the old relations, and create the agents capable of being the bearers of the new relations, and hence of the new class relations.

When new relations of production appear, they begin by exerting their action on the historically given productive forces. It is this action that *transforms* the productive forces, and imposes a *determinate structure* upon them. The productive forces that are transformed in this way are the productive forces *specific to* a new mode of production (to be precise, to the mode of production that results from the combination of relations of production and productive forces developed within these capitalist relations of production). Thus, capitalist relations of production took shape before machine industry; the latter develops under the domination of capitalist relations of production, to form the specifically "capitalist" *mode of production.* In the same way, socialist relations of production begin by exerting their action on historically given productive forces; it is through a definite transformation of these forces that the specifically socialist mode of production can be constituted.

The consequences of these propositions are numerous, but this is not the place to develop them. It is, however, necessary to stress two points:

(a) What we have just said signifies that the development of transitional social formations toward socialism cannot simply be based on a "reproduction" of the material conditions of production peculiar to capitalist social formations (though these conditions do form a "material base" for development).

(b) There is a particular mode of thought that mechanically relates the development of the productive forces to the transformation of relations of production and "thinks" the first term in a linear fashion (a superficial interpretation, which some of Marx's polemical formulations can appear to authorize), imagining that it is this "development" that "produces" a transformation in the relations of production. Such a conception turns its back on the real movement of history and can even have a negative effect on the development of transitional social formations.

These last two observations lead us to pose the following question: are not some of the characteristics of the techniques developed under the *domination* of capitalist relations of production the products of these same relations? Take, for example, the growth in the technical composition of capital, the *apparently* "necessary" growth in the size of units of production in order to obtain a reduction in costs (what contemporary economic ideology refers to as "economies of scale"). Far from being modalities of "natural laws of technique," are these not, quite simply, *social laws*—an effect of the domination of capitalist relations of production over the productive forces, quite concretely, an effect of the *laws of capitalist concentration and centralization?* There are many reasons for thinking that this is the case.

A positive response to this question involves considerable theoretical and *practical* consequences. It implies, among other things, that the importance purely and simply of techniques originating in the most industrialized capitalist countries (where centralization and concentration of capital have been pushed the furthest) can only contribute to the development of the productive forces in the importing countries on the condition that the same traits of concentration and centralization are reproduced in them—at the price of massive exploitation of the immediate producers (primitive accumulation on a gigantic scale).

For countries that have accomplished a socialist revolution, a positive response to this question is clearly of decisive importance. In particular, it implies that the importing or "reproducing" (or even "perfecting") of the proven techniques of the most industrialized capitalist countries can create an obstacle to the development of the productive forces, since these forces have characteristics that call for new relations of production and enable these relations to really open up a new stage of history by revolutionizing the productive forces. It does seem that, at the level of *political technique,* what distinguishes *Soviet* from *Chinese industrialization* (which is achieved under the slogan: autonomy, independence, and development through one's own resources) is a recognition of the necessity for *not taking* capitalist technique *as a model,* while at the same time deriving the maximum of what is utilizable from it in the construction of socialism. This is expressed in an *immense economy in the requirements for accumulation,* thanks to which the industrialization of China can be achieved without pressure being exerted on the standard of living of the peasant masses; on the contrary, this standard has been greatly improved, and is progressing steadily. In contrast, in the Soviet Union the technical line followed (which was determined by a set of ideological and political conditions) has led to the realization of an onerous "primitive socialist accumulation," whose economic and political consequences have been so considerable that, in the final analysis, it is the socialist character of the accumulation that has been compromised. Of course, these remarks do not mean that the *system* of the productive forces in China is already the product of socialist relations of production, but only that a particular *transformation* of the productive forces begins to take place under the domination of new relations of production. Only a precise and concrete study can bring to light the specific characteristics of this transformation.

At the level of the relations of labor, the separation characteristic of the "enterprise" as a capitalist form of existence of the unit of production is manifested by the fact that, at regular periods, workers can be dismissed from the enterprise and must then look for alternative employment. The fact that in the "socialist" countries relatively strict rules exist concerning dismissal and, furthermore, that the "labor market situation" is generally such that it is not very difficult to find alternative employment, does not modify the wage-labor character of the relations of the workers to each "enterprise." Consequently, the functioning of the enterprise ensures the *reproduction* of the *separation* of workers from their means of production.

At the ideological and political level, the form of existence of the unit of production as an "enterprise" also ensures the separation of workers from their means of production. This is achieved through specific *ideological relations:* the "authority" of management, the internal hierarchical organization of the enterprise, and the social division of labor that links the labor of organizing to "intellectual" labor on the one hand, and the work of execution to manual labor on the other. Of course, these ideological relations are *also* reproduced by the ideological institutions that prepare the workers for life in the "enterprises": the content and even the existence of the various "divisions" within education (such as those inherited from capitalism) reproduce these ideological relations, and thus, in their own way, subject the technical division of labor to the social division of labor.

Finally, the reproduction of the separation of workers from their means of production is likewise ensured by the *political relations* internal to the enterprises; the legal authority of management can invoke means of repression, can effect control from "top to bottom," and can apply sanctions in the same way.

These various relations are *partially* transformed by the existence of a workers' state, through the action of a *ruling* workers' party, and, in particular, through the role played by the workers' party and the trade unions *within* the enterprise. However, this rule can only be *partial,* since a real transformation requires, among other things, the substitution of new ideological and political relations for the old relations, that is, an ideological "revolutionization" of the workers, which makes them assert themselves as the masters of production. When this does not take place, the possession of the means of production is, in fact, held by the managers of the enterprises. In principle, this withholding is controlled by the *representatives* of the workers, but the relations between social forces may develop in such a way that the "representatives" of workers, in the state and in the party, tend to become identified with the managers of the enterprises, rather than with the workers—hence the crucial importance of an ideological revolution. This forms one of the "moments" in the "revolutionization" of the enterprises, of their transformation into another "form of organization" involving a different distribution of the functions of direction and control. Only a transformation of this kind can establish (along with other transformations that concern not only the enterprise) one of the stages leading to *new forms of socialization of labor,* and thus to *the elimination of the value-form from the process of production* itself.

Secondly, as we have already said, the character of the separation is concerned with the *relations between the enterprises themselves.* Here also, the intervention of the *value-form* and of *commodity exchanges* constitutes the index of this separation and the means for "overcoming" it in its very reproduction. As we know, this separation implies the functioning of enterprises as units of production that are simultaneously "independent of" and "dependent upon" one another.

2. The two aspects of the separation and their relations

In appearance, the two aspects of the separation that characterize the "enterprises" relate to different determinations; hence the illusion that "money" does not fulfill the same function in the relation of the enterprises with the workers (money as currency) as it does in its relations between enterprises ("accounting" or "scrip" money). In the Soviet Union, this illusion has even given rise to an effort which aims to institutionally "separate" these "two moneys." [2]

Such an institutional separation can only be illusory, since the *two moneys are only one:* they are simply two forms of existence of a single money, as is shown by the fact that they must *constantly* be "transformed into one another."

In actual fact, it is the very existence of the enterprise, and the character of the double separation that is inherent in it, which has as its counterpart the existence of money and its functioning under two complementary forms. The money that each enterprise has put into circulation, either for the payment of wages or for the purchase of means of production, must be "recuperated" by the enterprise through the sale of its products. In the Soviet Union, this is a necessity linked to what is called "control by the ruble."

However, under the illusory form of an "independent determination" of the intervention of money "within" enterprises (payment of wages) and "between" enterprises (buying and selling of products), something real *is indicated:* namely, that the *process by which these two forms of existence of money can be eliminated is not the same* (in spite of the fact that one form cannot be abolished without the other also being abolished).

The elimination of money from the relations between workers and units of production requires an ideological revolutionization, just as it requires a more advanced level of development of the productive forces. The elimination of money from the relations between units of production themselves requires the domination of the plan over the units of production. To bring about the disappearance of commodity relations, this domination must take the form of a social domination by the workers over the means of production; this must be the form of social appropriation of the means of production and products by the workers themselves, and, therefore, not simply a form of the *unity of labor at the level of a social formation,* but also a form of the *socialization* of labor.

If the plan does not take this form, its intervention only partially *displaces* the *separation* of workers from their means of production. In this case, the intervention of the plan does not allow *commodity relations* to disappear; the plan is then only *superimposed on these relations.* It simply sets up a form of intervention of the political level within the economic level, a form of intervention that is appropriate to *state capitalism*. Besides, state capitalism can function either under the aegis of a capitalist state or a workers' state; depending on which is the case—that is, depending on the class nature of the state—the effects of the plan are partly different. But in both cases—from the moment that there is a separation of workers from their means of production and a separation of enterprises—the plan only exerts its action *on relations that are partly commodity relations,* relations which put up a specific "resistance" to the plan itself.

COMMENTS

This resistance and the contradictions that result from it can be eliminated in two ways: either by making the plan an instrument for the "duplication" of commodity relations (this instrument then contributes, at its own level, to the reproduction of capitalist relations of production inherent in the existence of money, wage labor, and "enterprises"); or, by transforming the social relations, and thus also the character of productive forces that assure the reproduction of capitalist relations of production. In the first case, the "plan" is only the ideological double of the "market"; in the second case, it is an instrument for the transformation of social relations and for a social domination over the conditions of reproduction. However, such an instrument can only exist within *limits fixed* by the social relations and by the relations of class forces. Any attempt to go beyond these limits (which can only be known through concrete analysis and real social practice) necessarily leads to setbacks. Commodity relations cannot be "abolished," and a plan cannot be substituted for them; they are eliminated through adequate political action in which the plan is only an instrument, and certainly not the main one.

The functioning of commodity relations, articulated through the form of the enterprise, itself involves a series of extremely important effects, which we must now turn to.

3. *Some effects of the functioning of commodity relations articulated through the existence of enterprises and the state*

A primary effect is that the *process of production* continues to have the form of a *process* in which value undergoes a self-increment, since *labor-power* enters into this process as value having the capacity to produce value greater than its own. Consequently, the enterprise is the place where *capitalist social relations of production* are reproduced. The existence of these relations must obviously be radically distinguished from the existence of the *capitalist mode of production,* since this mode (like every mode of production) only exists if an ensemble of *corresponding* social relations exist *simultaneously.* If this is not the case, that is, if the social relations of production characteristic of a given mode of production only *combine with the social relations relating to another mode of production,* then we do not have a *mode of production* but a *form of transition.*

In the case that we are investigating, if capitalist social relations of production (which are reproduced at the level of the enterprise) combine with *socialist social relations of production* (constituted by planned relations that have specific characteristics), then the existence of capitalist social relations of production is not identified with the capitalist mode of production since these relations only constitute elements peculiar to the capitalist socioeconomic system, which are still present in a transitional social formation. When these elements are *dominated* by socialist social relations of production, we can say that the *economic base* of socialism exists.

COMMENTS

The *transition* between capitalism and socialism is *characterized* precisely by the presence of such capitalist social relations, and therefore by the presence of the *bearers* of these relations. The elimination of these elements coincides with the completion of the transition.

The propositions formulated here have as their departure point Marx's analyses of the presence of "bourgeois relations" in the course of what he calls the first phase of communism,[3] and in Lenin's remarks on the transition.[4] However, they do involve new theoretical developments. What is new is not so much the use of the concept of "capitalist relations of production" to characterize the nature of the wage-labor relations in the state enterprises (since this use is directly based on Marx's analyses of the concept of "variable capital"), but the use of the term "state capitalism." Consequently, it is a question of extending this concept.

This extension appears to be justified (1) by the existence of a system of capitalist relations of production articulated on state property in contemporary transitional social formations;[5] (2) by the capacity of this system to reproduce itself; and (3) by its capacity to *dominate* the other relations of production when it is not itself *subject to a politics* of suppression and transformation.

In this case, the use of the concept of "state capitalism" enables us to specify the concept of "capitalist road"; it also enables us to understand that this road can be taken at any moment by a transitional social formation. This is what happens when state capitalism's politics of suppression and transformation have been abandoned, since state capitalism has the capacity to reproduce itself and dominate the other relations of production.

Within a conceptual field that is defined in this way, the concept of "socialist enterprise" (a contradictory concept, as is the very object that it designates) refers to the "enterprise," in as much as it is the property of a workers' state. The concept of "enterprise" characterizes the form of relations that are established between producers and the means of production within a particular form of the unit of production. The concept of "state capitalism" designates the *system* of capitalist relations of production that are articulated within state property.

The system of state enterprises constitutes a form of existence of "state capitalism under the dictatorship of the proletariat" (according to a formula used by Lenin to indicate a mode of state capitalism that is less strictly subordinated to the state than to the state enterprises).[6]

To the extent that the workers' state dominates this system, it "suppresses" it; but the system nonetheless remains subjacent to the economic base of socialism. Even though it is subjacent, its effects manifest themselves in various ways, notably through *the commodity conditions of the reproduction of* the different fractions of social capital, and through the *bearers* of the *social relations* corresponding to this system, that is, at the level of the class struggle. If, as a result of the consequences of this struggle, the domination of the workers' state is compromised or weakened, state capitalism can become the dominant economic form. Note that only this form fully corresponds to the concept of state capitalism, since it rests on *state property.* It is a question here of a particular economic formation characteristic of the *imperialist stage,* and not of a "new" stage, which would be a stage "beyond" the imperialist one.

To understand its effects, this form must clearly be subjected to a specific *analysis.* The elements of this analysis that are available to us at the present time indicate that it is a form characterized by considerable *instability.* This instability is related to a tendency toward the *decomposition* of state property (it seems that the essential traits of the "economic reforms" that are being undertaken in the various countries of Eastern Europe can be analyzed in this way).[7]

From the preceding comments, it appears that the development of a social formation in transition to capitalism cannot be explained by the "development of the market." This development is only an *effect* of the development toward capitalism, and is itself determined by a reversal in the relation of social forces. Yet, such a reversal is not necessarily expressed in a "development of the market"; on the contrary, it can determine, at least in a temporary way, the "reinforcement" of state capitalism (clearly, this point cannot be developed here, but will be taken up in another context).

The domination of socialist relations over capitalist relations precludes the exploitation of the workers (the surplus-value produced by workers in enterprises becomes the property of the workers' state, which appropriates it and redistributes it in accordance with the requirements for the construction of socialism). But the existence of capitalist relations nonetheless does imply the *possibility* of restoring the exploitation of workers by those who control the use of the means of production. This exploitation can be undertaken as much by those who intervene as "possessors" of the means of production (the managers of the enterprises), as by those who are supposed to "control" them in the name of state property. The "conflicts," which can oppose one of these categories to another, are never anything more than secondary effects, since those who intervene in the name of state property are no longer the representatives of the immediate producers, but simply form a category of agents who exploit the producers—in other words, a dominant class.

COMMENTS

The point to be particularly emphasized in what has been said above is that it is *the wage-labor relation,* intervening in *commodity production* (production that has as its aim value and its increase) that constitutes a capitalist social relation of production. The existence of commodity relations is not sufficient to distinguish capitalist relations, since, as we know, commodity relations can fulfill various functions. They only become *relations of production* within the sphere of production. When they exist in this sphere, they enable the value-form to penetrate the process of production itself; this process then becomes a process in which value undergoes a self-increment.

A second effect of the functioning of commodity relations—and this is of fundamental importance in relation to our analysis—is constituted by the very *obstacles* this functioning puts in the way of the development of *social economic calculation.* These obstacles[8] occur under two forms.[9]

The first is constituted by the *ideological effect* of commodity relations, or, more precisely, by the *space of representation* within which *these relations are necessarily represented.* In turn, the existence of this space of representation develops a series of effects, which Marx designated by the terms "fetishism of commodities," "illusions," etc. These effects give monetary calculation a *consistency,* and in so doing, they bar the way to a real economic calculation.

COMMENTS

In addition, a whole series of "norms" that are bound up with commodity ideology are rooted in these representations: the norms of formal equality, of reciprocity, etc. This is the terrain that nurtures "bourgeois" legal ideology and "bourgeois" law.

The second form under which the obstacles to the development of social economic calculation occur is linked to the functioning of commodity relations and is, if we can use the term, "negative." It is constituted by an *absence of knowledge,* an absence *necessarily* inscribed in the functioning of any market, in as much as the market *establishes the relations between the different units of production in a way that is purely external.*

In effect, commodity relations only enter into relation with the units of production through the intermediary of their *products* and not through the intermediary of their *labor.* This labor is carried out within each unit of production, and therefore the different types of labor *do not directly confront* each other. It is precisely this character of commodity production which, within commodity production, makes it impossible to have a *real* economic calculation, a direct measure of the socially necessary labor-time. It is precisely this character that restricts the exchanging parties to monetary calculation, and that only makes an economic calculation possible for agents who, by not being inserted into commodity relations, are situated in conditions that enable them to really "penetrate" the different units of production and to have a knowledge of the processes that take place within them; however, this already implies a "revolutionization" of the units of production in so far as they are enterprises.

To sum up: within transitional social formations, at the economic level, the existence of commodity relations and capitalist social relations is bound up with the existence of enterprises. These "units of production" are such that they correspond to the structure of the productive forces and to the ensemble of social relations inherited from capitalism. They tend to reproduce these relations. The relations themselves can only be radically transformed through a *process of struggle,* which is economic, political, and ideological; consequently, this transformation can only occur as the *historical result* of such struggles being led to victory.

COMMENTS

The preceding comments once again raise the illusory (and eventually, under certain conditions, reactionary) nature of formulae of self-administration. At best, these formulae can enable *some immediate producers* to have at their command collective legal property ownership over some of the means of production (those belonging to the "enterprises" in which they work), but these formulae only result in dividing the workers into as many groups as there are self-adminis-tering *enterprises.* These enterprises continue to be linked to the market, and under these conditions the workers cannot really dominate either their means of production or their products, since this use is itself dominated by commodity relations. In other words, the problems that *self-administration* poses, through the intermediary of commodity relations, are problems that are *separate* from those of production, but which, nevertheless, do exert a decisive influence on the functioning of enterprises and on the (financial) results obtained by them. As a result, those immediate producers who are "in charge of" these problems are the ones who really *direct* the enterprises, simultaneously controlling both the labor process and the conditions for the reproduction of capital. This is the case even if these managers are "nominated" by the immediate producers. Moreover, all the characteristics of the social and technical division of labor peculiar to capitalism are reproduced in the "self-administering" enterprises. Only in a period of retreat—and then only provisionally and on condition that it does not serve as an ideological camouflage—can self-administration momentarily enable the workers to avoid the direct seizure of the means of production by a state bourgeoisie. In contrast, in a period of rising social struggles, self-administration can be a sort of "economistic trap" that encloses the workers within the limits of the enterprise, thereby restricting their horizons and hiding the necessity for a real domination by the workers over the means of production, and for a socialization of labor radically different from the one brought about through commodity relations.

In the course of the preceding pages, the emphasis put on the role of the enterprise as a matrix institution for the reproduction of capitalist social relations must not make us lose sight of the fact that, in contemporary social formations, there exist other conditions that ensure the reproduction of these relations.

(a) The existence of a world capitalist system

One of these conditions, whose examination would require too lengthy a treatment for it to be dealt with here, is the existence of a *world capitalist market* and of *capitalist social relations dominant on a world scale.* This point has been mentioned earlier;[10] in particular, this existence has the effect of making a part of the means of production enter into the process of production as *commodities,* whose determination of value is not known directly, since it is only known very indirectly, through its price. Furthermore, the dominance of the capitalist market and of capitalist social relations compels one part of production units to function for the world capitalist market. Certainly, the relative "isolation" of the units of production, which permits the *installation of a monopoly of external commerce,* does place some limits on the effects of the existing world capitalist market; however, to *limit* is not to *suppress* but only to *displace* the mode of action of the world market. Thus, under certain internal conditions, the pressure of the world market can be such that it gradually comes to dominate a growing part of production.

Furthermore, the existence of a world capitalist system is not only a source of "directly economic" pressure, but it is also a source of political and ideological pressure. This pressure is exerted, for example, on modes of consumption and on the forms of organization of the "enterprises." It tends to consolidate the enterprise and capitalist relations because, as a *capitalist institution,* the enterprise—as a place in which value undergoes a self-increment—necessarily functions better under conditions of capitalism than under those of transition, where it must give way to another form of the unit of production.

(b) The existence of the state and the state apparatus

In analyzing the action of contemporary transitional social formations and the conditions under which economic calculation can develop within them, it is impossible to neglect the problem of the state apparatus, under the pretext that it is not an economic problem. In actual fact, the existence of certain *political forms* plays a part in imposing a *separation* between the immediate producers and their means of production; consequently, it also contributes to the imposition of commodity relations within the sphere of production.

The scope of the questions that are posed here is such that we will only be able to deal with them briefly, taking as a departure point Marx's and Lenin's theoretical propositions on these questions.

Recall that what Marx called "modern state power" is, in his view, nothing other than "the bourgeois form of government." [11] The centralized state is a parasitic form,[12] which the workers' state cannot utilize. It must smash it and substitute for it a different political form. This is why Marx stresses that, in seizing power, "the working class cannot simply lay hold of the ready made state machinery and wield it for its own purposes," [13] and that it is necessary to smash and demolish this apparatus in order to substitute for it another apparatus *which is no longer,* strictly speaking, a *state power.*[14]

As is well known, Marx saw this *new political form* in the *communal constitution* as it emerged from the Paris Commune.

COMMENTS

Because the communal constitution has a noncentralist political power (although it does maintain some centralization), Marx saw in the commune "the transitory form" of the disappearance of the state, or, to use another of Lenin's expressions, "the transition from state to non-state." [15] It is for this reason also that many Marxist texts speak of "workers' power" rather than "workers' state," or put the term "state" in quotation marks when it refers to the *political form* of the working class. However, it has become established political usage to refer to this political form by the term "state" as well, thereby indicating that it is a question of a "particular type of state." This is the way that Lenin put it in 1917, for example, in his text "On the Dual Power." [16] He characterizes this type of Soviet "state" as "a power which is based on initiative coming directly from below, from the popular masses and *not from a law* promulgated by a centralized state power." [17]

For Marx, this new political form—which has not been invented but "revealed" by history—is a necessary form for what he calls "the economic emancipation of labour," [18] since it permits the abolition of "the standing army and the state functionaries," [19] and creates the conditions that enable the workers to "regulate national production through a common plan, thus taking it under their own control." [20]

However, the history that produced the communal institution has also produced (for reasons which cannot be analyzed here) other political forms of working class power, more centralized forms, such as those that were set up in Russia during the years 1917–1920.[21] This political form, imposed by historical conditions, was called by Lenin a "workers' state with *a bureaucratic deformation.*" [22] The existence of such a political form, as with the existence of the enterprise, plays a major role in the reproduction of capitalist social relations.

COMMENTS

It is in a speech given on December 30, 1920,[23] that Lenin characterizes the then existing Soviet state in the terms indicated above. He recalls that this characterization has been retained in the program of the CPSU(B), and he stresses its importance in order to demonstrate the necessity of trade union organizations for the working class, enabling it to defend itself against a state which "is not quite a workers' state." [24] Lenin's speech is directed against Trotsky's theses, which did not acknowledge that the workers' trade unions might have to defend the workers from a "workers' state."

This political form is destined to be transformed. It can either be "revolutionized," giving way to a less centralized, more democratic form that is closer to production. Or, its centralist traits can be reinforced, becoming increasingly separated from the workers and "ruling" them more and more, thus constituting an apparatus whose members form a "body" with its own internal rules of recruitment, in which the base is "responsible" only to the summit, on which its "fate" and, in the first instance, its development, depend.

In other words, this form can play the matrix role in "bourgeois" social relations. It can become the place where the means of repression directed against the workers are constructed, the place where the power to utilize the means of production and to dispose of its products is concentrated, and the place toward which the elements that are the social bearers of nonproletarian ideological relations converge, elements that are more "adapted" to tasks of repression, and to those of administration and planning without the control of the immediate producers.

The historical evolution of the state apparatus in the Soviet Union has been in this direction. It has produced a specific type of state apparatus, whose characteristics are found again in the state apparatus of the Eastern European countries.

Because this type of apparatus also *separates* workers from means of production, it necessarily sets up a particular form of planning and economic calculation, and it impresses a particular character on "social" property. This is precisely why the effects of this property cannot be analyzed without taking into account the concrete characteristics of the state institution that supports it. [25]

In effect, during the transitional period, the state (or a political form fulfilling the same functions in this respect) is the support for "social" property. This means that this property *is not social,* since it is exercised by the state "in the name of society." Thus, *even at the level of property, the immediate producers are separated from their means of production: they are only "proprietors" through the intermediary of the state.*

The real significance of state property *depends on the real relations* existing between the mass of the workers and the state apparatus. If this apparatus is really and *concretely* dominated by workers (instead of being situated above them and dominating them), then state property is the legal form of the workers' social property; on the other hand, if the workers do not dominate the state apparatus, if it is dominated by a body of functionaries and administrators, and if it escapes the control and direction of the working masses, then this body of functionaries and administrators effectively *becomes the proprietor* (in the sense of a relation of production) of the means of production. This body then forms a *social class* (a state bourgeoisie) because of the relation existing between itself and the means of production, on the one hand, and the workers on the other. This situation clearly does not imply that this class personally consumes the totality of the surplus-product, but that it *disposes* of this product according to norms that are class norms, norms that include an obligation to allow the market and the "criteria of profitability" to play a dominant role.

COMMENTS 1

The term state bourgeoisie, which is used here to designate this stratum, is justified by the *forms of separation* between the immediate producers and means of production on which its power depends. It is also justified by the *functions* that this class fulfills, the principal one being the *function of accumulation* that it carries out as an agent of *social capital.* This is why the problem of the personal consumption of this class is a relatively secondary question, as is the mode of accession to these functions, that is, the mode of entry into this class.

COMMENTS 2

Of course, in terms of the domination and control over the state apparatus, either by immediate producers or by functionaries and administrators, not only do two extreme situations exist, but there are also intermediate gradations. Consequently, movements in one direction or the other are possible. At this level, these movements form one of the essential characteristics of the transitional phase.

When the movement in the direction of the domination of the body of functionaries and administrators over the state apparatus has reached such a point (due to the development of political forces, as much within the apparatus of the state and party as outside them) that a movement in the opposite direction can no longer be anticipated—except through a rebellion of the masses—and when the masses cannot rely on the support of a part of the state management and the ruling party, we can say that the domination of the state bourgeoisie is completely installed, and that the transitional phase has been terminated by the restoration of capitalism.

On the contrary, when the ensemble of social relations has been profoundly transformed in the direction of a real social domination by the workers over the means of production and the political institutions, *state property* itself disappears, to give way to *social appropriation*. Clearly, this is a prospect whose realization presupposes a radical transformation of the world situation itself.

COMMENTS 3

If it is a question of the "restoration of capitalism" and not of the setting up of an entirely new class domination, it is—as we have seen—because the class domination that is reestablished in this way is tied to the domination of capitalist social relations, which still exist but which only occupy a subordinate place during the previous period of the transition as long as the state bourgeoisie does not dominate the political apparatus. The domination of the state bourgeoisie tends, fundamentally, to ensure a considerable extension of commodity relations and monetary calculation. Consequently, state property tends more and more to be merely a simple legal relation, which is not articulated in actual economic relations (planned relations playing a dominant role). These points cannot be developed here; they can only be developed in concert with a concrete analysis of the development that has taken place in the Soviet Union during the last ten years.

Consequently, state property is only something more than a simple legal relation to the extent that it corresponds to social relations that *dominate* commodity relations. This domination is one of planned relations, that is, of planned obligations that form the substance of a real economic plan (as opposed to plans that are "predictive," "indicative," etc.). Such a plan is the form of the *unity of labor,* to the extent that it enables the producers to regulate production in common and in so far as it is not a simple accompaniment, duplication, or reinforcement of commodity relations; in effect, only then is it the instrument of radically new relations and the primary form of existence of socialist social relations.

This leads us on to formulate a final set of comments concerning the relations of the state and its planning organs to the units of production. These remarks aim to clarify the effects on these relations of the functioning of "enterprises" as a form of existence of the units of production.

COMMENTS 4

A first and well-known effect consists of the imposition of the value-form on part of these relations. This form intervenes as much in the "calculations" of the planning agencies themselves, through the modalities of the fixing of the enterprises' planned requirements (requirements that are partly fixed in monetary terms), as in the state's centralization of the product of surplus-labor, since this centralization also takes place "in money," that is, in the form of "payments" made by the enterprises and destined for the state budget. (The value-form, money, the political form of the state, and the economic form of the enterprise thus constitute elements that reciprocally support each other.)

A second effect is concerned with the modalities of state control over the activity of the enterprises. The very organizational form of the enterprise, its internal structure, and the social relations that character- ize it tend to create an obstacle to the *concrete* control of its activity. At the same time, the existence of the value form and commodity relations (consequences of the functioning of the enterprises) allows for a control that is *abstract* and *external,* a monetary control that is carried out on the basis of the *balance sheet* of each enterprise, and on the basis of an examination of its *financial results.* The more commodity relations develop, the more state agencies are led to control the financial results and to interest themselves only in these results (which are expressed in budgetary "receipts").

In the most extreme case, the development of commodity relations can result in the planning agencies leaving the enterprises "free" (really or formally, it hardly matters) to elaborate the essentials of their "plans" for themselves, while requiring that these plans permit the enterprises to maximize their earnings as well as payments to the budget, with the reservation that an adequate "coherence" is maintained in these "enterprise plans." The role of the planning agencies then consists in controlling this coherence and in verifying whether the "criteria of maximization" are respected. In such a case, "control through money" is maximized, and the plan is no more than an accompaniment of commodity relations. It is this orientation that has been taken in the Soviet Union since the reforms of September 1965.

A third effect, which we have already indicated since it is intimately related to the preceeding two effects, is the opening up of a large field to *monetary calculations,* even at the level of the planning agencies. This tends to stifle the development of *economic calculation.* Obviously, it is not a question of a "direct" effect: the stifling of one form of calculation by the other is only an image since this "stifling" is always the product of a *politics,* that is, of an economic, ideological, or directly political class struggle.

COMMENTS 5

It is important to recall here, once again, that not only is there no rigorous *equivalence* at all between economic calculation and monetary calculation (this can easily be demonstrated),[26] but that "monetary calculation" is always a *pseudo-calculation.* It is based on magnitudes that are not the result of measurement, and its "results" are already entirely *inscribed,* not only in the dimension of magnitudes that are already "given" (this goes without saying, since it is the property of all calculation), but also *in the laws which determine these dimensions.*

Furthermore, this calculation does no more than "automatically" draw its consequences *from a given market situation.* Of course, this does not mean that this calculation serves no purpose. It *enables the laws of the market to function more rapidly;* consequently, it is not distinguished from these laws but is their *complement* or, if you like, their *extension.*

As a general rule, it seems that we can say that the monetary form of the relations between the state and the centers of production must develop all the more to the extent that these relations concern the *managers* of the enterprises as long as they dominate the immediate producers. On the other hand, the nonmonetary form of these relations, the concrete analysis of the labor process internal to the units of production, requires (if it is to be something more than a semblance or pious hope) the development of direct relations with the immediate producers, their participation in the elaboration of plans, and, therefore, a revolutionization of the enterprises.

The tendency to dominance of monetary relations, and to the absence of direct participation by the immediate producers in the elaboration of the plan, form two correlative effects of the *separation* of the workers from their means of production; they imply the development, not of socialist relations, but of capitalist relations, initially under the modality of *state capitalism.*

4. *State property and the plan*

It follows from the above that the form of the plan can correspond to:

(a) A duplication and an "accompaniment" of commodity relations

In this case, it is the commodity relations that are dominant. The workers are then entirely separated from their means of production: this implies that even at the level of the state they have been eliminated from power, and therefore that capitalism functions within the formal legal framework of "state property." As long as this framework continues to exist, we are dealing with state capitalism dominated by a state bourgeoisie; certainly, this situation does not prevent an "indicative plan" from being elaborated, but it does make it impossible to put real planning into operation.

COMMENTS

A comment and a specification are useful here. In the preceding formulation, a distinction is introduced between the "elaboration of a plan" (which is a practice that can be undertaken even when commodity relations are dominant) and "planning." As we know, this latter term indicates a complex social practice through which transformations that correspond to a political project are effectively realized in the field of productive forces/relations of production. The degree of correspondence between the real transformations and the projected transformations constitutes one of the indices of the degree to which planning is effective. Obviously, it is only one index. In actual fact, this "efficacy" of planning can only be made the object of indirect evaluations, notably on the basis of the "realization" percentages of the plans. Moreover, taken by themselves these percentages provide no information as to the real significance of the transformations that could be produced.

(b) The dominance of socialist relations over commodity relations

This can only really take place if the separation of workers from their means of production has, at least partially, been brought to an end. This presupposes that the workers occupy a dominant political and economic position, at least through the intermediary of a *vanguard,* ensuring the direction of the state apparatus and control over the units of production. In this case, the plan ensures the *unity of social labor.* Yet, the existence of commodity relations, as much at the level of enterprises as in the relations between enterprises and state agencies, signifies that this unity *is not yet that of socialized labor.* "State property" and "bourgeois right" form the framework for a *"state capitalism" dominated by the working class.* Capitalist social relations of production still exist, but they are placed in a subordinate position and combined with *planned economic relations that dominate them.* This *specific combination,* which is peculiar to the transition, is generally designated as corresponding to the existence of a *socialist "economic base."*

COMMENTS

The above propositions call for three kinds of observations:

(1) The concept of "vanguard," in fact, designates the ruling "workers'" party, but only to the extent that it is a workers' party in terms of its *social base,* in its *relations* with the *immediate producers,* and in its ideology.

(2) If such a vanguard does not exist, and, in particular, if the ruling workers' party does not have, or no longer has, the characteristics which make it a vanguard of the working class, then the *political and ideological conditions* which enable planned relations to be dominant over market relations *do not exist.* When this is the case, it is, indeed, possible to *formally* have a document that bears the name "plan," but this only conceals the absence of real planning. In effect, under these conditions, such a "document" cannot be based on a profound and *internal* knowledge of the units of production and the production processes that take place within them. Now, in the absence of this knowledge, no planning can be put into operation. Thus, what exists is an unstable combination of *commodity relations* and *administrative orders* (which the managers of enterprises more or less obey). The recent concrete experience of the Soviet Union and other "socialist" countries confirms that this is indeed the case. In the long run, this situation can only lead to the abandonment of such a semblance of planning and to the full development of commodity relations.

(3) The third observation concerns the expression, *"dominance of socialist relations over commodity relations."* The concept of "dominance" signifies that the reproduction of commodity relations does not

determine the fundamental characteristics of the reproduction and transformation of the system—relations of production/productive forces. In other words, when this is the case, commodity relations determine neither the *volume* of *accumulation* nor its *distribution* between the various *social spheres,* nor the principal social and material conditions ("techniques," for example) of production. Consequently, commodity relations only fulfill limited functions at the level of the everyday administration of the units of production, and they fulfill these functions under the domination of planned relations. It is in this sense that they are dominated.

These specifications relating to the concept of dominance are indispensable at a time when, in the Eastern European countries, the concept is used in a very particular sense in the notions of a "guided market," or "controlled socialist market." [27]

These notions allude to a reality entirely different from the one defined by the concept, "dominance of socialist relations over commodity relations," even though they *seem* to be "equivalent." In actual fact, these notions designate a political and economic practice in which the "market" (that is, commodity relations) plays the *dominant* role, while the role of state administrative requests is to *predict* what transformations commodity relations impose, in order to be in a position of optimal *adaptation* to these transformations. It is *not* the "market" that is "managed," but, rather, there is an attempt to exert control over the concrete conditions of the market's operation. For example, in the propositions of Ota Sik, it is a question of "self-guidance" based on "world prices" (and, therefore, on the basis of capitalist social relations) in order to determine the branches in which investment occurs and the techniques that must be put into operation.

(c) The presence of socialist relations on their own

In this case, the economic plan ensures the *unity of socialized labor.* Here we have a situation whose realization still appears distant at the present moment. It presupposes not only profound social transformations in the socialist countries, but also an end to the dominance of the capitalist mode of production as a world system.

These, then, are some of the analyses that appear to be necessary both for a better understanding of what has been termed the "survival" of commodity categories, as well as for a clarification of the conditions for an effective (and not simply an imaginary) elimination of commodity relations—conditions which are likewise those for a real development of "economic calculation."

Notes

1. On this point, see V. I. Lenin, *Collected Works* (Moscow: Progress Publishers, 1965), 27:323n; and particularly pp. 333–34. See also the analysis of the concepts of "socialization" and "stratification" in my book, *La Transition vers l'économie socialiste*, part 17, chapter 2.
2. See M. Lavigne, part 1, chapter 2, n30.
3. See the *Communist Manifesto* and the *Critique of the Gotha Programme*.
4. See, in particular, Lenin, *Collected Works*, volume 32, chapters 1 and 5.
5. Preobrazhensky was one of the first to account for the existence of this system, by using the notion of "socialist commodity system" (see *The New Economics*). This notion is inadequate since it only refers to the sphere of circulation.
6. It is well known that Lenin often used the term "state capitalism," particularly in the texts of 1917 and 1918 (where he simultaneously indicates both the system of relations resulting from nationalizations and the measures of state control), and in the texts of 1921 and 1922 (where he principally refers to the system of "concessions" given by the state to private capital, to the development of cooperatives under state control, to the use of "bourgeois specialists" in the state sector, and to the introduction of monetary and financial relations between state enterprises), but the use of this term is not systematic: it essentially has a descriptive character. As we know, this term is found again in the description of the "tendencies of state capitalism" or of "state monopoly

capitalism," in the texts that Lenin devoted to the analysis of contemporary capitalism, and to German capitalism in particular, during the same period. N. Bukharin also used the notion of "state monopoly capitalism" (in *Economics of the Transitional Period*), but for him this notion ultimately refers to the conception of a "single state trust," that is, to something very different from the system of enterprises linked by commodity relations, and functioning with the object of reproducing and increasing value.

7. I propose to analyze the meaning of these "reforms" in a later text.

8. I have already pointed out some of the aspects of these obstacles in chapter 1.

9. The following developments owe much to discussions I have had on this subject with Etienne Balibar and Yves Duroux.

10. See above, part 1, chapter 2.

11. See Karl Marx, *The Civil War in France* (Peking: Foreign Languages Press, 1966), p. 70.

12. What Marx is referring to here is "the centralised state power with its ubiquitous organs of standing army, police, bureaucracy, clergy, and legislature—organs wrought after the plan of a systematic and hierarchic division of labour. . . ." (*Civil War*, p. 64) It is this state that Marx is talking about when he states that "the communal constitution would have restored to the social body all the forces hitherto absorbed by the State parasite feeding upon and clogging the movement of society" (pp. 70–71), and when he describes it as a permanent source of corruption, with its "irresistible allurements of place, profit, and patronage. . . ." (p. 64).

13. Marx, *Civil War*, p. 64.

14. Speaking of the Commune, Marx says that its existence was no longer "a check upon the now *suspended* state power." (*Civil War*, p. 71; my italics, C.B.)

15. Lenin, *The State and Revolution*, in *Collected Works*, 25:432.

16. Lenin, *Collected Works*, 24:38–41.

17. Ibid., pp. 28–39.

18. Marx, *Civil War*.

19. In the first draft of an essay devoted to the Paris Commune, Marx puts it this way: "It begins the *emancipation of labour* . . . by doing away with the unproductive and mischievous work of the state parasites; by cutting away the springs which sacrifice an immense portion of the national product to

the feeding of the state monster on the one side, by doing, on the other, the real work of administration, local and national, for workingmen's wages." (Marx, *Civil War*, pp. 171–72)

20. Ibid., p. 73.

21. This other form of political power was put into operation during the Civil War. In 1920, the Ninth Congress of the Russian Communist Party admitted the necessity of this form. With regard to this, Lenin put it in these terms: "If we do not want to be guilty of sheer utopianism and meaningless phrasemongering, we must say that we must take into account the experience of the past, . . . that for the work of administration, of organising the state, we need people who are versed in the art of administration, who have state and business experience, and that there is nowhere we can turn for such people, except the old class." (*Collected Works*, 30:458)

It is this state apparatus that Lenin will qualify "workers' state with bureaucratic deformations" (see below), because of its hierarchical structure and the system of appointments that prevails in it. If it remains a workers' state during this period, it is because only the state *apparatus* is "bureaucratized," while the political power—which *dominates this apparatus*—is a workers' power, not exercised "directly" by the "whole of the working class" but by the vanguard of the working class, which forms the ruling workers' party. This party is, therefore, clearly linked to the masses, for whom it effectively is a political and ideological vanguard. It is the combination of the action of this vanguard, of the action of the apparatus of the soviets, and of the trade unions that ensures the domination of the working class over the state apparatus, and that enables the working class to hold political power.

When, in December 1920, Lenin describes the way in which the dictatorship of the proletariat is being carried out, he says, "What happens is that the party, shall we say, absorbs the vanguard of the proletariat, and this vanguard exercises the dictatorship of the proletariat. The dictatorship cannot be exercised, nor can the functions of government be performed without a foundation such as the trades unions. These functions, have to be performed through the medium of special institutions, which are also of a new type, namely the soviets." (Lenin, *Collected Works*, 32:20)

22. Stressed in ibid., p. 24. (The English translation reads: ". . . workers' state with a bureaucratic twist to it."—Trans.)

23. "The Trade Unions, the Present Situation, and Trotsky's Mistakes," ibid., 32:19.
24. Ibid., p. 24.
25. As we know, a concrete historical analysis cannot be limited only to social relations, but must also account for *institutions*. (On this point, see Lenin's comments in the April Theses, *Collected Works*, 24:32.)
26. The point of departure for such a demonstration is as follows: all monetary calculation is inscribed in a "system of prices" that is the result of historically given monetary expenditures and revenues that "correspond" to the material and social conditions of production at a particular time. If monetary calculation has a predictive character, it aims to produce the "optimal conditions" under which a particular result can be obtained. These "optimal" conditions are themselves expressed in monetary terms (in expenditures, or reports of receipts and expenditures). Consequently, they always refer to a system of prices: either the system existing at the moment of calculation, or a system "modified" by particular hypotheses. Such calculations cannot tell us very much about the strictly economic significance of the intended results, and the conditions of their realization; that is, they cannot tell us much about the transformation of the relations of production, about the development of the productive forces, or about the characteristics of these forces. The significance of such calculations is strictly limited to monetary magnitudes, which are the only ones present in the field within which these calculations are inscribed; however, this does not mean that the economic space can be reduced to the monetary field.
27. See the works of Ota Sik, *Plan and Market Under Socialism* (White Plains, N.Y.: International Arts and Sciences Press, 1967), and *Czechoslovakia: The Bureaucratic Economy* (White Plains, N.Y.: International Arts and Sciences Press, 1972).

Chapter 2

Unit of production and "enterprise"

The preceding analyses have clarified the role that enterprise (i.e., the ensemble of social relations that correspond to this existing form of the units of production) still fulfills within the reproduction of market relations and, more particularly, within the reproduction of capitalist social relations in contemporary transitional social formations. The term "enterprise" has thus been used to indicate a form of the production unit that is characteristic of the capitalist mode of production; the radical transformation of this form is necessary for the effective elimination of commodity relations.

These formulations clearly imply that the "unit of production" can have other forms of existence than that of the "enterprise." Although this point has already been referred to a number of times, it has not gone beyond the level of indication since the concept "unit of production" still has to be specified; in the same way, it is essential to deal more precisely with the existing forms of the units of production.

We shall not be able to deal with every aspect of these problems here; however, we must stop for a short while at this point—in the first place, to clarify the concept, unit of production.

COMMENTS

In the formulations contained in this text, I have substituted the terms "unit of production" and "economic unit" for those of "technical subject" and "economic subject," which were the terms used in previous texts (notably in my book, *La Transition vers l'économie socialiste*). I decided on this substitution because of the ideological charge that permeates the notion of "subject" and because of illusions concerning the "autonomy" of "subject" that this term evokes.

1. The notion of unit of production

The division of labor implies that the ensemble of labor processes on which social reproduction depends is divided up among a particular number of laborers. If the material and social conditions in which the laborers participate in labor processes are such that some of these processes form a general unity (ensemble) which regularly groups laborers and means of labor together so that all these processes are *directly interrelated* by being *separated from other processes*, we will say that the means of labor are acting as "supports" for directly interrelated labor processes, in the way laborers who put these means of labor into operation form "units of production."

Thus, the "material base" of the unit of production is constituted by an ensemble of means of labor serving in the *reproduction of determinate processes of labor*. Consequently, a unit of production exists as long as it reproduces an ensemble of labor processes with the help of an ensemble of means of labor. The existence of the "unit of production" through time is, therefore, nothing other than the existence of successive cycles of the same labor processes assisted by the same means of labor. Without wishing to spend too much time on this question, we shall note that:

(a) While there can be a change in the individual laborers who participate in successive cycles of the labor processes, the "unit of production" continues to exist. Thus, the unit of production is *distinct* from the "individuality" of *laborers* who face the means of production and put them into operation within the unit. Furthermore, these individual laborers themselves form a "collective laborer" whose "existence" is independent of that of the laborers who make up the collectivity.

(b) In the course of successive cycles, certain labor processes and means of labor can disappear and be replaced by others: nonetheless, the unit of production continues to exist from the moment when there is *no break in the cycles of reproduction of the labor processes;* in effect, when this is the case, these processes continue to be inserted in the same way within the division of social production, which itself also undergoes continual transformations while *reproducing itself.*

The result of this is that *the unit of production is itself reproduced through the reproduction of the labor processes.* This means that the labor processes are *not only* processes of labor but are *simultaneously processes of production,* since they *ensure the reproduction of the social conditions of their own functioning.* Consequently, they reproduce the *social relations* in which they are engaged, and they are concomitantly the effects and conditions of these relations. The unity of the labor processes and the production process forms the unit of production. In the absence of this unity of the two processes, we can have a "unit of labor" but not a unit of production.

COMMENTS

In the above text, the term "labor process" designates a "process between man and nature." As Marx stated, this process considered "abstractly" is an "individual" process whose "simple elements" are: (1) The personal activity of human beings (or purposeful productive activity—*Zweckmässig*) or labor, strictly speaking; (2) an object on which labor acts; and (3) a means by which labor acts.[1]

The labor process as it is historically given is not an "individual" process (since it is inserted within a division of labor). It is a process of *social* labor that is distinguished from the individual process by the *divisions* which the social character of the process introduces into the elements that intervene. The structure of the process of *social* labor has as an effect that it is also a *process of production* having its own "purpose."

This is why the distinction was made above between "labor process" and "process of production." The latter term designates a *double process:* the labor process (which "produces" use-values) and the process of production, *which is the process of reproduction of the social conditions* of labor itself.

Consequently, the process of production is not only a social labor process but also a *process of reproduction of its agents* and their respective *positions* and thus a *process of reproduction of relations of production;* from the social viewpoint, this reproduction is yet the *only form of production* (it is precisely this that Marx means when he says that in the capitalist mode of production, production "produces" capitalists and wage laborers).

The *process of social production* not only contains an immediate process of production (whose "base" is formed by labor processes) but other processes necessary for the reproduction of the social conditions of production, that is, the processes of circulation, distribution, and, consequently, *the relations of distribution* which form the "other side" of the relations of production.[2]

Every unit of production forms a *center* for the appropriation of nature. Within such a center, different labor processes are closely articulated; thus, every unit of production actually has the capacity to utilize its means of production, which it consequently *possesses.*

In transitional social formations, the means of labor that every unit of production within the state sector has at its disposal was either already at its disposal when it was nationalized, or has been *allocated* to it by the state (in practice, by an administrative agency of the state), or has been purchased by it.

A unit of production only exists (i.e., can only function) if it *actually disposes of* its means of production and can thus determine the *internal conditions* under which they will be used.

The products which "circulate" within each unit of production do not have to be bought or sold since, in practice, the different labor processes are not independent of each other but, on the contrary, "exercise control" over one another in a rigid or relatively rigid manner. Under these conditions, the "passage" of "products" from one labor process to another, for which they become the "raw material" (hence the "circulation" of these "products"), takes place under conditions that are strictly determined by the nature of the labor processes "controlled" by the unit of production, that is, by its "directing instance."

The control exercised by the unit of production, and thus by its "directing instance," over its means of production, objects of labor, and products (in so far as they circulate within the unit of production) is the consequence of objective requirements of labor processes themselves as they develop under *determinate social conditions*.

The technical division of labor and the division of social production require that the *different units of production enter into relations* with each other. These relations represent a *specific mode of articulation of different labor processes,* which are not as strictly related as those labor processes carried on within the same unit of production. The increase in the relations between units of production is the corollary of the socialization of productive forces.

The *forms of relationship* between units of production can be extremely varied. In particular, there can be stable ("organic") relationships whose *reproduction* ensures the formation of *complex units of production;* furthermore, this "complexity"—and the forms of relationship it implies—can be more or less considerable.[3]

Thus, because of the very nature of the labor processes carried out by different units of production, and also because of the regularity of the relationships between them, and because of the capacity (which results from this regularity and depends upon *technical, social, and political* determinations) of predicting with some precision the movements of products going from one unit to another, some units of production can form "complex units of production."[4] When this capacity to predict exists, the movements of products between the *elementary* units of production ("technical units" or, rather, "cells of production") that form a determinate complex whole can be *socially regulated in advance*. This may be done either by the *plan,* by a *directing instance which is common to* the ensemble of the elementary or "technical" units that form a complex whole, or by *one* of the elementary *units* of production that dominates the others; such a dominant unit of production then becomes a *crucial link* in social planning, and the latter then has no need to intervene in the "intercellular" movements controlled by this unit of production.[5]

In other cases, the movements of products between units of production cannot be regulated in a strictly a priori fashion, because the social conditions for a sufficiently precise prediction of the reproductive requirements of different units of production are not given nor is the capacity to satisfy these requirements except by direct relations between units of production.

COMMENTS

It is this situation that I described in chapter three of *La Transition vers l'économie socialiste*, when I wrote:

> We know that, given the present level of development of the productive forces, even in the most advanced socialist society, the process of appropriation *is still not a single process* totally dominated by society but remains a multiform process that is fragmented and divided up among a certain number of operational centers, and divided into processes for the appropriation of raw materials, which only begin to be capable of coordination on a social scale (through socialist planning); at the same time, we understand the necessity for exchanges between these operational centers, the real economic and social content of the different forms of socialist property, the necessity for socialist commodity exchange, and the role of money within the socialist sector, etc.[6]

The reader will have noted the change that has occurred between the problematic that this text involved and the problematic of the present analysis. The latter does not refer solely to "the level of development of the *productive forces*," but to the *social conditions* for a sufficiently precise estimate of the requirements for the reproduction of different units of production, and for the capacity to satisfy these requirements other than by means of direct relations between units of production. However, these social conditions do not depend solely on the "level of development of the productive forces" but on the effects of the *social relations of production* and *other social relations* (political and ideological).

This change of problematic is made necessary by the analyses presented in the course of previous pages of this text. However, it does not modify the *description* that can be made of the *effects* of contemporary forms of the *division* of social production.

When the structure of the production processes that develop in the different units of production and the social conditions for the enlarged reproduction of these processes are such that the latter cannot be regulated and articulated a priori through a *social power* external to the units of production concerned, then it is necessary—to the extent that this is the case—that these units of production themselves have at their disposal the power to establish more or less variable relations between them. Such a power does not necessarily exclude a social power external to the units of production and which fundamentally regulates the units' activity.

2. Economic units, enterprises, and the existence of the value-form

When the action of social relations and the structure of productive forces result in some of the units of production having at their disposal the power to establish more or less variable relations between units (to direct their production toward such and such another unit, or to procure their means of production from within some other unit), they not only have the capacity to utilize their means of production, but they also have a certain *power of disposal over their products.* Therefore, at one and the same time, they take part directly in the *process of immediate production* and in other processes that constitute the *process of social production,* the processes of circulation and distribution. Under these conditions, these units of production form "economic units of production."

The economic units of production not only have the capacity to *utilize their means of production* (the "possession" of these means), but they also have the power to *dispose of their products* and, within certain limits dictated by the social conditions of reproduction, to dispose of their *means of production.* If this power is exclusive, it corresponds to *property ownership* (to a relation of property); if it is *subordinated and limited* by a *dominant power,* then it corresponds to a particular form of *possession.*

COMMENTS 1

The above proposition, as much as the previous ones, makes it apparent that the concrete use of the concepts of "property" and "possession" raises a number of difficulties. Clearly, these are related to the fact that these concepts in their present state are not sufficiently "developed," and, thus, differentiated.

It seems that in order to overcome these difficulties it would be necessary to distinguish between *types of property* and *types of possession.* These types refer, on the one hand, to the degree of socialization of the productive forces (which allows more or less generally unified production processes to be brought under control) and, on the other, to *social relations* and, primarily, to the *relations of production* (and thus to the effective *social control* exercised by economic units or determinate political authorities over processes of production and circulation), but also to *legal forms* (i.e., to recognized and sanctioned "rights").

Within each type, it would be necessary to distinguish *degrees* of capacity or power, degrees that are related to the state of the productive forces, which determines a more or less extensive "technical control" (thus, for example, this technical control is still relatively feeble in agriculture, which makes it difficult to make precise estimates with regard to production, demand for labor-power, manure, means of transport, etc. in this sector). Degrees of capacity or power are also related to inequalities in the development of social control: the control exercised over particular links—for example, over particular economic units—occasionally makes possible effective control over a whole series of other units; as a result, these units, in fact, lose part of their "property." The different forms of "integration" of the economic units thus realize many variations of degree.

In actual economic practice, the variations in the types of property and possession and their unequal development are the sources of specific *contradictions* that can block or slow down the development of the productive forces, limit the efficacy of certain relations of production, act as a restraint on their enlarged reproduction or transformation, and even provoke inversions in their movement. All these points would have to be developed.

COMMENTS 2

The economic units in question in this text are economic units of production (thus also of productive consumption). Obviously, economic units of consumption (e.g., families or "consumer collectives") also exist. The problems posed by the functioning of these units, by their insertion into the process of social reproduction, are not examined here. Consequently, in the following pages the term "economic units" refers to units of production.

A *double connection* is set up between the economic units, which are related as units of production and as economic units.

The relations that connect economic units to other *economic units,* to *economic agents,* or to *economic organizations that depend upon political power,* are concerned at one and the same time, but under different modalities, with the "concrete labor" and the "abstract labor" consumed within each relation; they are thus concerned with the *two aspects of the same labor* that simultaneously reproduce the *material* and the *social* conditions of production.

COMMENTS

The term "economic organization that depends on political power" remains a descriptive notion. In relation to transitional social formations, it refers to extremely diverse institutions: planning agencies, agencies for the "material distribution" of particular products (e.g., the system by which technical materials are supplied in the Soviet Union), state collecting agencies,[7] financial and banking institutions, etc. The traits that are common to these organizations are that they are situated outside the sphere of material production; under the conditions of the transition, their relations with the economic units *do not necessarily assume the equivalent form* (they can operate "unilateral transfers"); their activity is not primarily determined by the *relations of production* which they can be subjected to, but by *political relations.* Concretely, they are "institutional relays" for the action of the political level. The theoretical concept or concepts corresponding to this descriptive notion still have to be elaborated, but it has not been possible to do this here.

In the capitalist mode of production, as we know, the double appearance of labor takes the form of the *reproduction of social capital as much in "material" as in "value,"* as Marx pointed out in the analysis of the schemas of reproduction.[8]

In capitalist social formations, this "double reproduction" has taken place entirely within the *value-form,* and in the premonopoly stage it is carried out almost entirely under the *form of equivalence;* thus, at the level of each economic unit (which is then an "enterprise"), the values which "emerge" from this unit under the monetary form are exchanged for an "equivalent magnitude" of products and labor-power, and, at the end of each cycle of production, the values which "emerge" from the enterprise under the form of products are exchanged for an "equivalent" sum of money, which will, in turn, be used to purchase new products and labor-power of an equivalent magnitude, etc. Of course, all these "exchanges of equivalents" mask the exploitation of labor-power by social capital. This exploitation is concretized in the profits realized by the enterprises—profits which tend to be redistributed in proportion to the fixed capital within each enterprise, in spite of the deviations from this "norm" that are imposed by the functioning of the market.

The form of equivalence continues to prevail in the monopoly stage of capitalism since, at the level of immediate representation, products are "valued" at neither more nor less than their prices. However, the *reciprocity* form which was the double of *equivalence* in the premonopoly stage, tends to dissociate itself from the latter. The most visible form of this dissociation is formed by the *subsidies* paid to certain enterprises; another form of this dissociation is constituted by the *transfers* and *levies* raised by state (or corporative) economic organizations on the receipts of the enterprises. These "movements of value" do not have the form of *reciprocity* and, because of this, they also tend to lose the form of equivalence, although the space of representation peculiar to the capitalist mode of production tends to make equivalence appear under a new form: that of the "restoration of equality" between enterprises or, eventually, between economic agents.

Beyond these forms, what we are concerned with is the *reproduction of the conditions of production:* it is a question of ensuring the reproduction of the *material and social* conditions of production which, *under the domination of the relations of production and the action of the bearers of these relations* (that is, the class struggle) do not impose reproduction "pure and simple," but—simultaneously—*reproduction and transformation of the economic and technical units,* and, therefore, determinate transformations in the concentration and centralization of capital, in the distribution of the social product, and in the structure of the productive forces (and, therefore, in the division of social production).

In transitional social formations, the functioning of enterprises as a form of *economic units* implies, in the initial stage, the temporary maintenance, though under a transformed form, of the modalities of reproduction of material and social conditions of production analogous (but not identical, as we shall see in a moment) to those which characterize capitalist social formations.

Therefore, during this "initial" stage, the means of production, even if they are nationalized, still function as "social capital," and the *essential character* of the relations of the economic units to each other and to the laborers still assumes the form of equivalence (this, then, is the "economic base" for the maintenance of the "bourgeois right" Marx talks about), so that the economic units are still "enterprises."

However, from this "initial stage," the domination of the working class and, consequently, the existence of a workers' state and its nationalization of the means of production enable some of the *social conditions* of reproduction to be profoundly transformed—relative to their existence in capitalist social formations; this is why, earlier on, we spoke of analogous conditions, but not of identical conditions. More thoroughgoing transformations in the conditions of reproduction require either that the economic units no longer be enterprises, or that their functioning be "revolutionized," which presupposes profound transformations of ideological and political relations.

COMMENTS

The above formulation, in which it is a question of "economic units that are not enterprises," clearly refers to a particular form of existence of economic units. In the present state of social practice, it seems that in transitional social formations the two categories of economic unit that correspond to such a form are, on the one hand, the people's communes, in as much as they are a political and economic unit, and, on the other, the units of production (notably the industrial) that function in these communes. A study of the conditions in which these units function would enable us to clarify more concretely the characteristics of such forms of existence of "economic units."

Note also that if, earlier on, it was stated that at an "initial" stage economic units still function as enterprises, this formula must be understood in relation to the historical experience of the Soviet Union, where this has been the case. It was not shown that this is necessarily so; although in social formations where the form of the enterprise is the general form of existence of economic units, it is difficult to see how it could be otherwise.

3. The functioning of the "enterprises" in the conditions of transition, and the characteristics of plans

The points we are going to take up now refer to economic units in so far as they are enterprises. In effect, the practice of social formations in transition concerning this form of existence of economic units is extensive enough to be reflected upon theoretically. However, while these points are very much a "resumé" of what has been said in the course of the preceding pages, they are formulated in a way that is partly new in order to make the specific conditions of the functioning of enterprises in transitional conditions clearer.

We have seen that when economic units function as "enterprises," they take part in social production and circulation through commodity categories. Consequently, among themselves, the enterprises maintain *commodity relations*. The existence of these relations is determined at one and the same time by the relative "independence" of the labor processes that are carried out within them, and by the ensemble of political and ideological conditions that are dominant.

The existence of economic units as "enterprises" implies not only the existence of commodity relations but also money and prices; hence the necessity for the enterprises to balance their monetary receipts and expenditures and for the monetary form generally taken by the enterprises' contribution to the funds for social accumulation ("payments to the budget"); hence, reciprocally, the budget contribution to the enterprises' accumulation ("budgetary donations") can also assume a monetary form.

However, beyond this reproduction of commodity relations and monetary forms, the existence of a workers' state and of state ownership of the means of production produces (since this ownership of property corresponds to a real relation of production) more or less *profound transformations* in the social conditions of reproduction. As we have seen, the immediate form of this transformation is the establishment of *planned economic relations* which dominate *commodity relations* and assume the form of an "imperative economic plan."

These planned economic relations are one of the specific forms taken by the intervention of the *political level* in the *economic level* under conditions of the transition toward socialism. It is a question, therefore, of a specific form of socialist social relations. This form is destined to develop along with the consolidation of the ensemble of these socialist relations and to retreat if capitalist relations of production, which are present in transitional formations, develop to the detriment of socialist relations.

This does not mean to say that a simplistic correlation can be established between the detailed and thoroughgoing character of an economic plan and the degree of dominance of socialist relations of production. What matters is not the "plan" as document but the ensemble of *real social relations*. It is these, and these alone, that ensure the *effective domination* of planned relations over the reproduction and transformation of the conditions of production. This domination is manifest in the *effective* transformations that the economic plan *imposes* on social relations and on the structure of productive forces.

The term "impose" signals, at one and the same time, a *nonconformity* between objectives of the plan (and the evolution that will give rise to commodity relations) and a certain "conformity" between the *transformations* that will effectively take place in the system of productive forces/social relations and their equivalent objectives.

The extent to which this "conformity" is more or less considerable essentially depends on the political and social conditions under which the plan is *prepared* and *put into operation* (that is, upon the real place of *immediate producers* and their representatives in these processes). The "technical conditions" for preparing the plan and putting it into operation are only secondary to this primary dependency; these conditions are always subordinated in their effects to political and social conditions. If the latter do not correspond to the requirements of real planning, then the plan cannot *dominate* the transformation of social relations and the structure of productive forces. The plan is then the means by which a simple "semblance" of planning can be achieved. Under the cover of this semblance, a domination is exercised, which is not that of the direct producers.

COMMENTS

The term "semblance" is used here to underline that, under the conditions indicated, the "plan" does not function as it is supposed to: the effects it produces are not those that have been explicitly "sought after," and only very exceptionally do they conform to objective interests of the dominant class. In actual fact, the existence of legal state property in the absence of the political domination of the working class has generated illusions: illusions that are related particularly to the effectiveness of economic plans that assume a "fetishistic" character.

However, as we have already indicated, the real inefficacy of economic plans elaborated and "operationalized" by a class other than the working class can, in the absence of a fundamental change in the relation of social forces, only lead to an open dominance of commodity relations, and thus either to the collapse of a "semblance" of planning, or to the transformation of the plan into a simple reduplication and reinforcement of the conditions for the reproduction of *commodity relations* and relations of exploitation.

When planning is not a simple "semblance" and, consequently, when there is some "conformity" between actual economic and social transformations and "planned" objectives (this "conformity" being not only expressed by the "percentages of plan realization," but also by the nature and rhythm of transformations), then there is both *dominance* and enlarged reproduction of planned economic relations.

As we have said, the *dominance* of planned economic relations is manifest in a nonconformity between actual economic development and the development that would be brought about by commodity relations. Consequently, this dominance gives rise to a "reversal" of commodity relations and their effects.

At the level of each "enterprise," this reversal is manifest in a more or less considerable separation between the processes of production that develop within each enterprise and the processes which have developed under the dominance of commodity relations. This "separation" concerns not only the *labor processes* (what is materially produced) but also the *social conditions* of production (the prices, wages, sources of supply, and the "recipients" of production).

Thus, *contradictions* develop between the conditions for the reproduction of commodity relations and the conditions for the reproduction of planned relations. The analysis of these contradictions and their movement still remains to be done. Here we can only point out a number of their manifestations.

Concerning the enterprises that are actually subjected to an economic plan, the contradictions in question are particularly manifest in the fact that (contrary to what happens in enterprises subject to the immediate domination of commodity conditions of production) the processes that develop are not dominated by the tendency to *maximize the value* of the fraction of social capital they possess; to put it in descriptive terms: obtaining a maximum profit is no longer their "objective." Here the *break* with the conditions for the reproduction of capital under the immediate dominance of commodity relations is clear.

COMMENTS

It could be thought that "analogous" phenomena exist in the industrial and financial groups whose functioning characterizes monopoly capitalism, and that this is even more clearly the case when the tendency to state monopoly capitalism develops. In appearance, this is correct. Indeed, under conditions of monopoly capitalism, alongside enterprises which function to maximize their profits, there are others that are condemned to operate at a loss or at rates of profit inferior to those which could be obtained if certain conditions had not been *imposed* on their functioning (either by other enterprises or by state regulation). This "analogy," which cannot be analyzed here, indicates the growing contradiction between capitalist ownership of the means of production and the increasingly social character of the productive forces; however, it does not go beyond this, since the *politics* to which some of the "enterprises" are actually subjected *is itself dominated by the search for profit,* which means that the "losses" or "periods of no return" imposed on some of the fractions of social capital aim at ensuring the most favorable conditions for the production and appropriation of surplus-value by the most powerful industrial and financial groups. Obviously, this cannot be systematically proved here, since it requires an analysis of contemporary capitalist social formations, which is not our object.[9]

As a point of information, note that one of the questions that ought to be examined here is that of the "displacement of the limits" of the "enterprise"; this question is raised precisely by the existence of industrial and financial groups.

In transitional social formations, this break can produce a series of effects—either at the level of the functioning of economic units or at the level of the economic ensemble.

At the first level, these effects can be specifically concretized (since commodity relations continue to reproduce themselves) in the necessity to "subsidize" certain economic units—those that do not cover their monetary costs by equivalent receipts, and whose social conditions of reproduction are, consequently, not permitted by commodity relations. In certain cases, the break with conditions for the reproduction of capital under the dominance of commodity relations can go still "further" and be concretized through transfers carried out "in kind." The limits imposed on the extension of such operations are those that oppose the ensemble of social relations. The essential fact here is that, under conditions prevalent during the first phase of the transition, the bases for *monetary calculation*—as much at the level of economic units as at that of the ensemble of the entire social formation—cannot be completely dislocated since a real *economic calculation* is still impossible; on the other hand, if all possibilities for calculation were absent, this would seriously compromise the enlarged reproduction of conditions of production.

COMMENTS

The attempts made in Cuba, primarily since 1966–1967, to "disregard" monetary calculation, in a situation in which the conditions for a real economic calculation were not given, have been accompanied by a serious dislocation of the conditions of reproduction. Concretely, this is evidenced by the realization of a mass of investments that it will only be possible to use to a very limited extent in production, and which, therefore, will not be able to be reproduced (vast areas of land were cleared, planted, forested, etc. and these will not be able to increase social production to a sufficient extent to ensure the land's maintenance on the basis of this increase in production, i.e., the purchase of tractors, spare parts, and fuel that this maintenance requires). At the same time as these investments are realized, old equipment cannot be renewed, which means that the reproduction of this equipment is no longer ensured. In the case we are considering here, this dislocation of the conditions of reproduction is partly concealed by the massive imports made possible through credit, originating as much from the "socialist" countries as from the capitalist countries of Western Europe, principally France and England.

At the level of transitional social formations, the break with the conditions for the reproduction of capital under the dominance of commodity relations leads, among other effects, to the transformation of the laws of *price formation.* These can no longer correspond uniquely to the requirements of the reproduction of commodity relations since they must also correspond to the requirements for the reproduction of planned relations. This proposition has considerable implications, which can only be indicated here. It means, in particular, that the system of *planned prices* must be related to the objectives of the economic plan, and, consequently—to put it in descriptive terms which require theoretical elucidation—that these planned prices must simultaneously "reflect" the comparative, *politically* assessed social cost and social utility of the different types of production, and express them in "monetary magnitudes"; hence the profoundly contradictory character of the system of planned prices and the considerable difficulties in its elaboration. These difficulties have not yet been theoretically overcome, which implies that existing (or previously existing) systems of planned prices—through which economic units enter into relation with each other and ensure, at least partially, the reproduction of their own conditions of reproduction—have an essentially empirical character.[10]

These, then, are just several of the problems posed by the reproduction of the conditions of production of economic units when the *commodity relations* in which these units are engaged combine with *planned economic relations* when these latter *dominate* the former.

It is important to go on and make three essential observations (which take up and complete some of the propositions put forward above).

(1) The *dominance* of planned economic relations over commodity relations is clearly only the effect of the dominance of the political level of the social formation over its economic level, which is to say that "planned economic relations" *correspond to dominant political relations* that can themselves only be imposed as the effect of a *determinate political domination*. This political domination can only be, as we have seen, that of the *immediate producers*. In the absence of this, "planned economic relations" existing simply as a result of state property, for example, do not really dominate commodity relations; moreover, under these conditions, the "plan," which forms the "official summary" of these relations, retains only a "semblance" of planning.

(2) The crucial index of the *dominance* of planned economic relations over commodity relations is a certain "conformity" between the transformations that take place in the field productive forces/relations of production and the "objectives" of the plan. Obviously, this "conformity" is only significant if the economic plan contains real objectives and not simple "estimates" that the actual movement of the economy can more or less "confirm."

(3) These two propositions do not imply that the domination of immediate producers is necessarily and exclusively asserted through the existence of a set of planned economic relations, the "official summary" of which is an economic plan. In effect, the dominance of a system of planned relations can only be established if, beyond the domination of immediate producers, particular economic, political, and social conditions are given. Thus, if the effective dominance of planned economic relations over commodity relations implies the political domination of immediate producers, the converse is not necessarily true. Consequently, the real economic relations that develop within the framework of *legal state property* are not always the same. This is why state property

only forms an effective economic relation when it is "manifest" through planned economic obligations.

To summarize: *state property,* in as much as it is an *economic* relation, corresponds with planning and planned obligations; while *possession* by the production units of their means of production and products corresponds to these units' control over their means of production and to direct relations (not necessarily commodity relations) between these units.

On this basis, we can put forward the following propositions: to the *relations* of property and possession (whose *combination constitutes one form of property*) there corresponds a combination of two economic practices (and thus of two modalities of the "practice of production"); these practices are "planning" and the "administration" of "enterprises." Clearly, the precise content of these relations and practices is never given once and for all since it is dependent on ideological and political relations and, in the last instance, on the level of development of the productive forces.

The *duality* of state property and possession by the economic units implies that the development of each of these relations can enter into *contradiction* with the development of the other. Under determinate political and social conditions, it is through this contradiction that the struggle between the socialist and capitalist roads develops, that is, the struggle between the two antagonistic classes, bourgeoisie and proletariat.

COMMENTS

It is now time to point out, once again, a serious ambiguity that can (and actually is) brought to bear upon the concepts of "planning" and "state property." This ambiguity is a "historical effect" of the practice of planning in the Soviet Union. Here, for concrete political reasons, this practice has clearly had a centralist character; although state property has essentially been that of the *Union* of Soviet Republics or of *Republics.* Yet, what characterizes *planning,* in general, is not such a *centralization* (the latter refers to what Lenin, criticizing Trotsky, called the "bureaucratic deformation" of the Soviet state[11]), but a *real, a priori coordination* of labor and production processes, which restrains the operational field of commodity relations. Furthermore, as we have seen,[12] this coordination does not necessarily take the form of a "centralized plan"; it can also assume the form of a "superimposition of intercoordinated plans" that ensures a socially controllable articulation of the production processes. To this form corresponds a *system of planning* in which *state property,* held by regional or local *political units* (e.g., the popular communes) *dominates the simple possession* of the economic units; these units "coincide" with the political units, or they are subordinated to them. This domination relegates the *administration* of the economic units and the reproduction of commodity relations to a subordinate place.

Even when state property plays the dominant role, this dominance can be more or less effective; thus, the contradiction, state property / possession by the economic units, must constantly be *controlled.* If, in practice, this is done (implying not only political but also ideological, and consequently, technical and scientific conditions) then the strengthening of state property is paralleled by increasing socialization of productive forces; the social formation then develops toward socialism, that is, toward a real social management of the economy.

On the contrary, if this contradiction is not properly controlled, state property, instead of growing stronger, tends to disappear. It tends to become more and more formal, while possession by the economic units tends to be transformed into an effective, total, and complete property ownership. In this case, the evolution toward socialism is not achieved. Rather than *an increasing social direction of the economy*, it is, on the contrary, the *increasing role of the law of value* that asserts itself.

A development that turns the social formation away from the direction of socialism necessarily implies other transformations, as much at the economic as at the political level, since the increased role of the law of value also involves the development of its effects on the social division of labor and on the relations of distribution; the strengthening of the division of labor between those who direct the activities of economic units and the direct producers follows from this increased role.

Clearly, our object is not to study the modalities and consequences of such a development, but, rather, to analyze the conditions and forms of *predominance* of state *property* over the *possession* of economic units.

Notes

1. See Marx, *Capital*, 1: 177–79, and 531–34; *Le Capital*, 1:180–82; 11:203.
2. On these points, see *Capital,* 3: 832n, and 877–84.
3. This problem has been studied by Isy Joshua, "Organization and Relations of Production in a Transitional Economy (Cuba)," in *Problemes de Planification*, November 1967, No. 10.
4. On this point, see the developments in chapter 2 of my work, *La Transition vers l'économie socialiste*, especially p. 77n.
5. This point is also dealt with by Joshua, above.
6. Bettelheim, *La Transition vers l'économie socialiste*, pp. 146–47.
7. The term, "state collecting agencies" refers to agencies which, in the Soviet Union, are in charge of "collection"; that is, their task is to centralize the deliveries of particular agricultural products. "Collecting agencies," then, can be concerned with the sale of products by particular producers, with the standard or compulsory deliveries of these products, or with payments in kind, etc.
8. On this question, see "Les Schemas de la reproduction du capital chez Marx," in *Problemes de Planification*, February 1967, No. 9.
9. On this point, see Paul Baran and Paul Sweezy, *Monopoly Capital* (New York: Monthly Review Press, 1966).
10. I have dealt with some of the aspects of this problem in chapter 6 of my book, *La Transition vers l'économie socialiste.*
11. Lenin, *Collected Works.*
12. Ibid., 32:24.

Chapter 3

Planning and the predominance of state property

The predominance of state property over the possession of the economic units is basically achieved by means of an economic plan whose characteristics are preemptory. Consequently, this plan is the principal instrument for the social direction of the economy.

Such a plan determines the development rhythms of the different economic and social activities, and, therefore, of the various types of production and the use to which they are put—particularly the distribution of production between accumulation and nonproductive consumption. It also enables the transformation of production relations and of the productive forces to be controlled. Thus, within the limits of existing productive forces, such a plan determines not only the character of the labor processes and the production carried out within technical and economic units but also a number of the relations between these units.

COMMENTS

If this is not the case, that is, if the labor processes and production are basically not determined by the plan, then the *possession* exercised by the technical and economic units over their means of production and products is transformed into *property,* in the sense of an actual relation of production (this is the sort of development that the Yugoslav economy has experienced). This transformation does not preclude the intervention of a sort of indicatory planning or a "guiding" of the economy, but then this only plays a secondary role in the sense that, in this situation, it is the law of value that exercises the decisive *regulatory function*. We will come back to this question later.

If the economic plan is in a position to effectively determine a number of relations between the economic units of production, it is, of course (as was pointed out previously), because these units do not *exclusively* have the capacity to establish economic relations with each other by virtue of that very *duality, property possession,* which characterizes a certain "state" of the productive forces and relations of production.

It is this duality that gives rise to the *possibility* and, from the point of view of the development of the social formation toward socialism, to the *necessity* for an intervention by the planning instances at the level of relations between economic units of production.

The *modalities of this intervention* can be extremely variable. They are determined concomitantly by the structure of the economic level and by the character of the dominant ideological/political relations. The *combination* of these relations and the contradictions that develop among them determine the *periodization* of the transition, which does not have a linear form.

At the economic level, the regulatory power that constitutes state property develops to the extent that a more regular and predictable articulation is established between the processes of production controlled by the economic units. Such a development enables *social institutions* (which initially take the form of "state-controlled organizations"), as distinct from economic units, to establish relations with these units, and to control their utility from the point of view of economic, social, and political development.

In this way, *planning* can *intervene concretely* at the operational level, not only in an *abstract* and general manner, but by controlling "economic levers" (such as prices, monetary investments, etc.). This intervention directly contributes to the progressive elimination of the value-form and to the reduction of the operational field of the law of value.

The social institutions that can intervene in this way represent a section of the "planning organizations"—those that intervene at the operational level. Such organizations can be the *relay stations* for a *central planning agency.*

The various organizations and planning agencies can only fulfill their functions effectively if they are in a position to know what the major processes carried out within the different economic units are, to estimate the changes that can be introduced into these processes and their modes of combination, and to evaluate (in quantitative terms, if possible—hence to "calculate") the social results expected from these various possible combinations. In this way, these agencies play the role of "centers for calculation and social distribution of labor and products."

With the growing socialization of the productive forces and the increasing dominance of socialist relations of production, the capacity to establish connections between economic and technical units in a way that is socially effective can be increasingly concentrated at the level of the planning agencies and closely related to the various types of collective labor; this corresponds to the development of a real *social appropriation.*

1. *The relations between politics and the economic level in social formations in transition between capitalism and socialism*

The form of the duality, property/possession, produces another extremely important structural effect, which we must now deal with, namely the effect of the domination of politics over the economic level.[1] Due to this effect of domination, the economic level no longer enjoys the *relative* autonomy that it has in the capitalist mode of production, primarily in its competitive stage.

COMMENTS

The domination of politics over the economic level is, of course, *also* characteristic of the "later stages" of the development of social formations toward a real *social appropriation;* however, our object is not—and cannot be—the as yet unforeseeable *forms* that this domination can assume; our object is constituted by the *contemporary* problems of the transition. Nevertheless, one observation can be made here: it is essential to distinguish between the dominant role that politics retains, even in these "later stages" of the development of social formations, and the intervention of the *political level* (of the state and the law), which must have a tendency to decline. If this is the case, it is because the *ideological* is also the *site of a* crucial *political practice.*

Within the specific structure of social formations in transition between capitalism and socialism, one of the manifestations of the effect of the *domination of the political level* is formed precisely by *putting into operation a politics* which transforms the relations of production and develops the productive forces. The most complete form of this politics is economic planning.

The domination of the political over the economic level clearly does not mean that in the last instance the latter ceases to be determinant, but means rather that the economic level is determinant through the intermediary of the political level. The relations between the two levels are not directly *visible* due to the specific type of complexity that characterizes the structure of transitional social formations.

As in other cases, but under other forms, this complexity produces effects of dissimulation and inversion, from whence comes the illusion that the visible movement of perceptible appearance (*Wirklichkeit*) constitutes the real internal movement (*wirkliche Bewegung*), that is, the internal connection of the processes.

Here again, this connection can only be grasped through *analysis.* This explains the fact that, as long as the visible movement is incorrectly analyzed, the real internal movement[2] really remains unknown. When this is the case, a distinction between the role that the political and the role that the economic level plays, or can play, is only established in a partial empirical manner that is often inadequate.

To be more exact, without an *analysis which is to be concretely applied to the ensemble of the social formation* (that is, to its economic, political, and ideological levels), it is impossible to *understand* clearly the role that the economic and political levels must respectively fulfill in order that the social formation develops toward socialism.

Thus, the specific structure of the relations between the political and economic levels, an essential aspect of which is formed by the duality, property/possession, can generate two sorts of illusions:

On the one hand, "economist" and "legal" illusions that regard the "social" character of state property as given for all time, considering it to be identical to a relation of production, which is always active, thereby *tending to reduce the role of the political level* under the pretext that its interference with the economic level would be "arbitrary."

On the other hand, "subjectivist" and "voluntarist" illusions which tend to identify the *dominant* role of the political level with a sort of role of *determinacy* in the last instance. Voluntarism and subjectivism are particularly characteristic of economic plans that are not formulated on the basis of a rigorous social and economic analysis.

COMMENTS

The inadequacies of social and economic analysis are themselves dependent upon the relations of class forces, as much at the economic level (for instance, the very fact of the specific "opacity" of the enterprises, or the "cover-up operations" for which some of the agents of production are responsible) as at the ideological and political levels. This particularly concerns the ideological positions of the class of economic and political managers.

The extent to which voluntarism can develop in transitional social formations is obviously related to the dominant role of the political level in these social formations.

Voluntarism exists when the intervention of the political is pushed beyond the limits within which this intervention can be *effective,* that is, beyond limits that can be followed by expected effects. These limits are not given once and for all but depend on the ensemble of social relations. When they are exceeded, the intervention of the political level becomes inadequate and produces, in part, effects other than those that were sought after and which can even be the opposite effects of those sought after. Thus, production stagnates instead of advancing; the productivity of labor fails to increase; the relations between the branches of the economy develop in an opposite direction to the one expected; market relations, instead of retreating, develop, for example, under the form that has been called a "parallel world," a world that exists as the "double" of the "official world."

In the same way that economism tends to "fuse" the political and the economic level, voluntarism tends to "reduce" the economic to the political level, practically ignoring its existence, its laws, and, in the last instance, its determining action.

Contrary to current opinion, economism and voluntarism are not only political or ideological "currents." Obviously, they do produce such currents, but in transitional social formations they are rooted in specific forms of fetishism of social relations.

Economism has its roots in illusions that are linked to the existence of the value-form. Voluntarism has its roots in the dual character of state power during the transitional period (which is at the same time both an economic and a political power), and in the dominant role of this power.

The double character of state power generates the tendency to make a fetish of state power (in the same way that kinship relations are fetishized in other social formations). If there is no rigorous analysis of real relations, the consequences of such fetishization can be felt as much at the level of rulers as at that of the masses; when this happens, representations, ideological relations, and aspirations develop that can have extremely negative effects on the development of the social formation in the direction of socialism.

The struggle against economism and voluntarism demands, therefore, an analysis of real relations and the formulation of limits within which the action of the political level is really effective, since these limits are never "given," but can only be known through *scientific experimentation, critical analysis* of past actions, and struggle against subjectivism. This struggle requires that "lessons be drawn from past errors in order to avoid repeating them," i.e., that criticism and self-criticism be constantly carried out.

Clearly, the possible consequences of voluntarism are not only located at the level of "determining unrealizable targets for production," "investment," or "consumption." They can also be constituted through the introduction of "organizational forms," that is, explicit relations between agents in the production process that do not correspond to actual relations. In this case, these organizational forms are more or less ineffective, and the economic system functions partly as a result of the existence of other relations, which are more or less hidden by the first. We then have one of the forms of existence of what has been termed a "parallel economic world."

As a result of their "unexpected" effects, the inadequate forms of political intervention can react on previous forms of intervention. We must pause a while here to examine this question, particularly since the *obscuring effects* that develop in this way can, during a given period, increasingly limit the possibilities for economic and even monetary calculation.

2. The "obscuring effects" associated with inadequate forms of intervention: an example of these "effects"

When the question of "obscuring effects" is raised, a problem appears which, although often described as being one of the "instruments" of planning, is, in actual fact, a problem of the *forms of intervention* of the political in the economic level.

One of these forms of intervention is constituted (as long as the structure of the economic level requires it) by a *system of planned prices.*

An inadequate analysis of the structure of the economic level (and particularly of the role that the value-form necessarily plays at a certain stage) can easily lead to the illusion that this form of intervention is "not necessary." This can result either in the *planning of prices being abandoned,* in prices being arbitrarily fixed, or in a recourse to "instruments" that can be less adequate than correctly fixed prices, e.g., the introduction of administrative measures for the distribution of products when other forms of intervention would be socially more effective.

Among the secondary effects of inadequate forms of political intervention in the economic level and, therefore, forms of the relative inefficacy of this intervention, is the tendency for the state apparatus to develop to an excessive extent in a fruitless effort to master processes that are not successfully controlled for want of operating with suitable resources.

In turn, such an expansion of the state apparatus, of the number of its agents, of their "authority," and the extension of these repressive functions makes the *very knowledge of real economic phenomena more and more difficult.* The state apparatus intervenes between the political direction and economic and social reality. It puts pressure on this direction, and it *forms a screen.* This "screen" not only conceals reality, but it tends to play the role of a "mirror" that reflects the image the political direction wants to see, while the agents of the state apparatus develop *their own interventions* (which are *also* political interventions but correspond to another politics than that of the direction).

COMMENTS

When this movement develops beyond a certain point, it can, in actual fact, break up the unity of political power. Some of this power can then, in reality, be exercised by the *agents of a "capitalist politics"* who direct a greater or lesser number of central or local organizations, units of production, and ideological institutions. Here we have one of the *social bases* for the development of a *"parallel world,"* which entails, little by little, the formation of a *"second power."*

The "obscuring effects" brought about by inadequate forms of intervention can also lead to opposite consequences of those outlined above, particularly under the influence of *economism*. In this case, because of the inefficacy of the intervention of the political level, this intervention tends to be renounced. This can then mean the disappearance of state property, because this only exists economically through the real and effective intervention of the political level within the processes of production and reproduction. Without this intervention, state property constitutes a simple juridical superstructure to which the real relations of production correspond less and less.

It is precisely the existence of the *value-form*, particularly *in the process of production* and, through this, the existence of capitalist relations of production, especially the wage-relation, that make possible the "retreat" of the political level's intervention and the *resurgence of a market economy*. The dominance of commodity relations then necessarily leads to the dominance of capitalist relations of production.

At the level of economics, the possibility of reconstituting the capitalist mode of production has its root (as has been emphasized earlier) in the form, specific to the transition between capitalism and socialism, of the noncorrespondence between the relations of real appropriation and property relations. This noncorrespondence expresses the fact that the relations of real appropriation are only partially transformed (since their radical transformation is related to a radical transformation of the labor processes and their articulation), whereas the relations of production have already been profoundly "revolutionized."

As we know, the productive forces always play a *determinant* role in the last instance, while the relations of production play a *dominant* role: it is the character of these relations (and if there is a plurality of relations of production, it is the character of the dominant relations of production) that distinguishes the transitional direction in which a determinate social formation is involved.

Characteristic of every transition is the "advance" of particular dominant relations of production over the productive forces. To the extent that the latter have not themselves been transformed under the action of dominant relations of production, the transition is incomplete. The dominance of relations of production requires precise (but variable, according to the types and stages of the transition) modalities of *intervention* of ideological and political levels. Thus, the transition from the feudal to the capitalist mode of production brought to light a whole series of interventions ("reforms" of religious ideology and corresponding ideological institutions, the emergence of new "moral rules," political revolutions) that had to accompany the emergence of capitalist relations of production and ensure their dominance and consolidation.

Similarly, in the course of the transition toward socialism, the dominance of socialist relations of production, and the transformation attendant upon this dominance of the relations of real appropriation (essentially those that are reproduced within economic units), depends upon the intervention of other instances of the social formation within the economic instance. With regard to the content and forms of this intervention by the ideological and political levels, they themselves depend upon the state of productive forces and on relations of the social and ideological forces. The outcome of the struggles that develop at these levels thus constantly determines the development of *transitional social formations,* and this is so as long as the infrastructure can still allow capitalist relations to play a dominant role.

The above argument explains how the setting up of the dictatorship of the proletariat, under its initial forms, only permits the first elements of socialist relations of production to be introduced and that the struggle for an increasingly profound socialist transformation of the relations of production, and of social relations in general, must necessarily be continued.

To summarize, we can state that social formations in transition between capitalism and socialism are characterized by a particularly complex structure of their different levels, by specific forms of action of these levels on each other, and, consequently, by a certain instability. It is these very characteristics which, under the conditions of transition between capitalism and socialism, provide distinct "terrain" both for "voluntarist" and strictly "economist" practices, from which follow the darkening effects that we have been concerned with above.

3. *The fundamental economic laws of social formations in transition between capitalism and socialism*

A crucial effect of the complex structure we are analyzing, and more particularly, of the specific effectiveness of the political level that characterizes this structure, is that *the value-form cannot appear there without the law of value necessarily making its appearance as a regulator of the processes of production and reproduction of capitalist relations.* This happens because this *regulatory action* of the law of value is the effect of a structure characterized by a particular *form of unity* (which is now absent) of private property and private appropriation. This form of unity, which characterized the capitalist mode of production, has as its counterpart the complete *separation* of producers from their means of production.

On the other hand, the structure of the economy in transition between capitalism and socialism is, as we have seen, characterized by a particular form of noncorrespondence between property relations and relations of appropriation. The *former* are relations of *"social" property,* which enable the laborers to dominate the means of production through the intervention of the *political level.* The *latter* are still the relations of a real appropriation that is "private," in the sense that it is carried out within centers for the appropriation of nature that are *separated* from each other, and which can only be gradually *united* through a profound *transformation* of the material and social conditions of production.

COMMENTS

Marx describes this necessary *process of transformation* in the following terms:

> The working class knows that they have to pass through different phases of class struggle. They know that the superceding of the *economic conditions* [my emphasis—C.B.] of the slavery of labor by the conditions

of free and associated labor can only be the progressive work of time. The transformation that must be carried out is not only a transformation of distribution, but, beyond this, a new organization of production, or rather, the setting free of the social forms of production as they exist in the present organization of labor (engendered by modern industry), by tearing them away from the trammels of slavery, from their present class character, and, finally, requiring the harmonious coordination of these forms on the national and international level.[3]

One of the manifestations of the noncorrespondence between the relations of property and appropriation is, as we know, the *superimposition* of state ownership of the means of production[4] on the possession of these same means by the economic units that put them into operation—hence the duality, property/possession.

As a result of this *duality,* the social institutions that are "bearers" of state property can determine the principal tasks of the different economic units and the modalities of their relations. They can do this all the more adequately when the necessary political and ideological conditions are realized—conditions which have been specified previously.

COMMENTS

The social institutions that are the "bearers" of state property are, on the one hand, institutions that are "external" to economic units (for example, the planning agencies that operate under the control of political power) and, on the other, politico-economic units that coordinate the activity of the production units subordinated to them. To the extent the activity of these units of production is also concerned with economic units (of production or consumption) that do not depend on the same politico-economic unit, it is essential that a social institution "external" to the economic units intervenes, in order to ensure a coordination of activities that is advantageous to all the units. Such an institution is necessarily either a political or an ideological institution.

Under conditions in which the tasks of economic units are determined by social institutions, state property can intervene as a *relation of production.* If this relation is dominant, then it is no longer the law of value that dominates the reproduction and transformation of the conditions of production but another law, the *law of social regulation of the economy.* This law constitutes the mode of appearance (specific to the transitional economy) of the action of the political on the economic level, under conditions in which the value-form exists. It is the specific law of the *reproduction* and *transformation* of relations of production of economies in transition between capitalism and socialism.

This law is itself the product of the particular complexity of the structure of transitional social formations. It is due to this specific complexity that two distinct structural effects and, thus, two structural laws develop and combine: these are the *law of value* and the *law of social direction of the economy.* In effect, the latter can only operate on its own when the conditions under which commodity relations exist have disappeared. As long as this is not the case, that is to say, as long as the law of value has an operational field, the operation of this law is combined with that of the law of social direction; it is the effect of this combined action that is indicated here by the expression, "law of social regulation of the economy."

In other words, in the transitional period, where the law of value still makes its appearance, the law of social direction of the economy appears under the modified form of *the law of social regulation.*[5] The latter thus represents the result of the conflict and the combination of two antagonistic laws (the law of value and the law of social direction of the economy).

COMMENTS

Other formulations of economic laws of the transitional period, notably by Stalin and Preobrazhensky, have already been put forward in the works cited previously. The formulation proposed here seems preferable to us, in that it clarifies the *conflict* that exists between the law of value, the law of social direction, and the effect of the combined action of these two laws. It is useful to recall here, since it generally seems to have been forgotten, that Marx, in the first draft of his essay, *The Civil War in France,* approached this problem. He deals with it (in a descriptive way) in the sentences immediately following the passage previously cited.

It [the working class] knows that the present spontaneous action of the natural laws of capital and landed property can only be replaced by the spontaneous action of laws of the social economy of free and associated labor, following a long process of development of new conditions. . . .[6]

The "long process of development of new conditions" is that which develops in the course of the transitional period. During this period two types of laws confront one another and their effects combine, principally under the form of the law of social direction of the economy, on the one hand, and under the law of value, on the other.

Note that, in the final editing of the same text, Marx speaks of a "common plan" by "the ensemble of cooperative associations," as a result of which they take "national production" under "their own control."[7]

When the conditions under which the law of value functions have disappeared, the transitional period is complete; the *law of social direction of the economy* is then dominant on its own, while the duality, property/possession, has disappeared, and a *process of social appropriation* under the direction of the immediate producers asserts itself.

COMMENTS

In the above text, the expression "law of value" is used in the traditional sense (i.e., in a narrow sense); it thus indicates the specific form taken by the *law of distribution of social labor as a function of the requirements for the reproduction and transformation of relations of production* in social formations where capitalist relations of production exist (formations in which the value-form is present in the process of production itself, where "prices of production" play a role). It is essential to be this precise because the term "law of value" is sometimes taken in a broad sense to mean the law of distribution of social labor.

In relation to the above, it is essential to remember that the value-form leads, as Marx said, "an antediluvian existence." It is, in effect, present within "precapitalist" social formations, just as it is present in the course of the transitional period; however, it is only when the capitalist mode of production is dominant that the law of value (in the narrow sense) is also dominant and, consequently, that the latter governs the reproduction and transformation of the material and social conditions of production.

In social formations that are not capitalist but in which the value-form is present, without having penetrated the process of production, the "law of distribution of social labor" *peculiar to the mode of production that dominates these social formations* combines with the effects of commodity relations; hence the rather frequent illusion that the "law of value" could also intervene in these social formations, but in a "different way" than when the capitalist mode of production is dominant, and that, consequently, there could be "several laws of value," notably that of the capitalist mode of production and that of "simple commodity production."

The domination of the law of social regulation of the economy is obviously not "spontaneous." By its very nature, this domination requires the intervention of the political level, and this is only effective if the *contradiction* between the law of value and the law of social direction of the economy is *handled adequately.*

This contradiction itself constitutes the development (and, therefore, the transformed form) of the contradiction between *the mode of appropriation* and *the mode of property.* To put it more precisely, it is the product of a particular combination of property, possession, holding of the means of production, and disposal of the products. The *effects* of this combination do not only depend on the economic instance, but also upon the political and ideological instances. Similarly, the transformation of this combination is not only dependent upon the growing socialization of the productive forces, but also on transformations that take place at the political and ideological levels.

4. *Supplementary comments on holding, possession, and property*

We have already mentioned that it is necessary to distinguish between two different types of capacity and power to dispose of products and means of production and that, within each type, there are degrees or levels of capacity or disposal; we also said that, for the moment, and within the limits of this work, it was impossible to go any further with our research on this point. Therefore, the following formulations must be seen as incomplete and provisional, as intended only as guidelines for a more profound analysis.

We propose to use the term "holding" of the means of production to indicate the *relation of the immediate producers* to particular means of production, in so far as these means intervene *directly* in the labor process in which these immediate producers participate.

"Possession" will indicate the *relation* of particular *agents of production* (whether they are immediate producers or not) and, therefore, the relation of the economic units they control, to the means of production functioning in these economic units up to the extent that these agents *dominate* both the labor processes in which these means of production are used and the *material conditions of this reproduction*. If there is an identity between the holders of the means of production and the bearers of the relation of possession, then there is a *unity* of holding and possession, under the *form* of possession.

"Property" will indicate the relation of particular *agents of production* (and thus of economic units or social institutions they control) to the means of production functioning within units of production that are controlled in this way, up to the extent that these agents dominate both the *processes of production* where these means of production are used and the *social conditions of their reproduction*. If there is an *identity* between the bearers of the relation of property and the relation of possession, then there is a *unity* of property and possession *under the form of property*. When the agents of possession or of property are not the immediate producers, the latter are *subjected to* relations of property and possession under the form of *separation*.

COMMENTS

These different relations are represented as relations between the categories of agents and the means of production. This is their immediate appearance, which can be directly shown. However, we know that this appearance conceals something else, which is the profound reality of that appearance, namely knowledge of the relations between the agents themselves. In effect, if the various relations above are immediately relations between agents and material elements of production, they are *essentially relations between the agents themselves,* that is, *social relations of production.* This is because these are the *social conditions* that not only *place* the different categories of agents into determinate relations with the elements of production—into relations that are relations of adherence for some and relations of exclusion for others—but also, and above all, *replace* them in the *same relations.* Consequently, these relations are not "circumstantial" or "accidental" but *socially determined and socially reproduced.* This social reproduction passes through the moment of the *distribution* of products. It is this that enables us to say that the *relations of distribution* are only the reverse of relations of production.

The "domination" of processes of labor or production by the possessors and the owners of property in the means of production does not necessarily mean that they "control" these processes. Domination implies the capacity of a class of agents to act upon particular processes, thereby modifying their structure and articulation. Control implies that the agents who modify particular processes in this way subsequently achieve the results that were aimed at. Clearly, such a control is relative; the degrees of this relativity are the degrees of "effectiveness" of the agent's action.

The control of the processes (and also, therefore, of their results) depends on the development and state of the productive forces and upon *the structure of the field, relations of production/productive forces.* Only a particular structure of this field (corresponding to the development and state of the productive forces) enables the *social process of reproduction* to be operated upon effectively. The greater the degree of socialization of the productive forces, the more does the control of the different individual processes of production itself depend upon control of the general unity of the social process of reproduction. Economic and social planning leads to the control of the social process of *reproduction* and to the control of the *transformation* of material and social conditions of production. This social control is dependent not only upon "economic conditions" (which concern the field, productive forces/relations of production) but also on political and ideological conditions.

To summarize, then, holding, possession, and property indicate the functions effectively fulfilled by particular classes of agents (or by the institutions controlled by these classes) with regard to the processes of labor or production; consequently, these indicate the *relation of these classes* both to the *means of production* operative within these processes and to the *immediate producers* who participate in them, and thus to the relations between these classes themselves, at the level of production and at the level of the conditions of reproduction.

The *unity* of the labor and production processes (these processes being only *two aspects of the same process*) accounts for the fact that possession and property cannot be "mechanically separated." In a concrete situation, their place can only be determined by a *differential analysis;* furthermore, within the real movement of a social formation, possession and property are subject to *displacements;* these are related to modifications produced at the *different levels* of the social formation and, consequently, to the effects of the economic, political, and ideological class struggle. Thus, the plurality of powers that corresponds to property can give rise to *dissociations*—particular categories of agents holding one type of power and another category of agents holding another type of power. In the same way, again, a category of agents who were owners of the means of production, can—without the intervention of "economic" modifications that are immediately "visible"—be "expropriated" of all or a part of this property because they fall under the political and ideological domination of another class of agents. Of course, this expropriation will also manifest its effects at the "economic level," but these effects can only appear with a "displacement"; the transformations that take place at a determinate level develop, in effect, in the "particular time" of this level.

COMMENTS

The problem of *dissociation* of the plurality of powers that corresponds to property cannot be dealt with here. Nevertheless, it is essential to stress that it has considerable importance, as much from the viewpoint of the *dissolution* of a mode of production as from that of the *transition* from the dominance of one mode of production to the dominance of another. In capitalist social formations, the functioning of joint stock companies gives rise to a series of dissociations of property from the enterprises, various categories of agents being bearers of distinct powers. To the extent that the distribution of these powers is *unstable,* these various categories of agents do not form distinct social classes but one and the same class. Similarly, in transitional social formations, when the agents who are bearers of state property have acquired an autonomy in relation to the immediate producers, they form a state bourgeoisie, and the different powers that correspond to this state property can be dissociated among different categories of agents: directors of enterprises, directors of trusts, managers of economic administrative bodies, managers of ministries, planning agencies, etc. Therefore, as long as the distribution of powers among these agents is unstable, the latter form distinct categories within the same social class.

It follows from what has been said previously that the property of the workers' state (in as much as it is a relation of production) indicates the effective role that state institutions subject to the control and direction of immediate producers fulfill in relation to the processes of production. The modalities and the *effectiveness* of this control can be variable. One of the essential problems of the transition to socialism is to ensure such a transformation of forms of this control and direction that the latter are increasingly *consolidated*. This consolidation cannot be the result of a spontaneous process; on the contrary, it requires a *constant struggle against the tendency toward the separation* of the functions of control, direction, and execution. This tendency is itself inscribed within the ideological relations that are reproduced by *institutions* (economic, ideological, and even political) inherited by societies dominated by nonlaborers, since these institutions are not, and generally cannot be, immediately "revolutionized" and managed by laborers.

Consequently, it is only when a *general unity* of economic, ideological, and political *transformations* ensures a *growing control* by the laborers over the means of production and products that the transition to socialism has effectively taken place. Such a general unity of transformations leads to the development of a process of *social appropriation,* carried out under the direction of the immediate producers, and thus to the deployment of the *law of social direction of the economy,* which constitutes a fundamental law of the developed socialist economy. Its intervention implies putting a "direct economic and social calculation" into general operation; this economic calculation, which does not pass through the "detour" of the law of value, is the type of economic calculation that Engels indicates in the text cited at the beginning of this work.

Having made these comments, we can now go on to put forward a number of propositions concerning the problem of the economic laws of the transitional period.

5. *Concerning the economic laws of the transitional period*

Our aim here is not to enter into a discussion of the overall problem of the economic laws of the transitional period. This would largely take us away from the principal object of our reflection. In effect, such a discussion would call for an examination of the various formulations that were previously put forward with regard to the economic laws of socialism. Therefore, we will limit ourselves here to a number of observations relating to the formulations presented in this text.

It follows from these formulations that what we have called the "law of social regulation of the economy" constitutes a particular transitory and unstable form of combination of the law of value and the law of social direction of the economy. The place which can and must be left to the law of value and the way in which the value-form can be put into operation socially can only be determined by a *concrete analysis of the objective conditions of this combination.*

As we have seen, one of the modalities of social implementation of the law of value is constituted by the formation of *planned prices.* Such prices, if they are to play the role expected of them (that is, if they are to play an active role in the socially directed transformation of the field, productive forces/relations of production), must, in the first place, express *not the requirements of the law of value but those of the social direction of the economy*—that is, to put it concretely, the requirements of the economic plan, or, more generally, of *economic politics.*[8]

This latter proposition means that, in the transition to socialism, politics must be in command of economics and, therefore, that the *distribution of social labor* is not dominated by the requirements of the reproduction of capitalist relations of production (which, while fulfilling no more than a subordinate role, are still present in commodity relations, the wage-relation, and the form of the enterprise) but by the requirements of the construction of socialism. This construction implies the increasing control of immediate producers over production and also, therefore, the development of production in terms of present and future needs of producers. What is meant by "needs of producers" is obviously not only what is necessary for "individual" consumption and for productive consumption but also what is necessary for the growth of production and for everything that is needed for the consolidation of the workers' state, including what is needed on the international level—the totality of these requirements and needs being *evaluated politically.*

When this is the case, the law of value fulfills no more than a secondary function: in particular, it is not this law that determines the direction and form of accumulation. This means, among other things, that the planning of investments is no longer subject to a criterion of "profitability" (financial or monetary). For this criterion is substituted another—that of *political and social effectiveness*—which has an entirely different character.

COMMENTS

Thus, through a different type of analysis, we rediscover a number of previously cited conclusions from Stalin's work, *Economic Problems of Socialism in the USSR,* particularly the following conclusions: ". . . the law of value cannot (under the Soviet regime) function as the regulator of production." [9]

"Totally incorrect," too, is the assertion that in "the first phase of development of communist society, the law of value regulates the 'proportions' of labour distributed among the various branches of production";[10] hence the following formula:

"Profitability" [11] must be considered not "from the standpoint of individual plants or industries, and not over a period of one year, but from the standpoint of the entire national economy, and over a period of, say, ten or fifteen years. . . ." [12]

It is this "profitability," *which is neither a monetary nor a financial profitability,* that I indicate here by the term "social and political effectiveness."

Before coming to some of the implications of the above analysis, I should add from the viewpoint of economic and monetary calculation, that I have put forward the concepts of the laws of "social direction" and "social regulation" because these concepts seem to me to give a better account of the real movement than does the notion of the "law of balanced development of the national economy" (a notion that is presented in Stalin's text).

In actual fact, a balanced development is only a consequence of a correct social regulation; it is not the direct and necessary product of a structure but the result of a *political action made possible* (but not only possible) *by a particular structure.*

6. *Law of value, economic calculation, and monetary calculation*

If the law of value (in the precise sense of a "law governing the distribution of social labor as a function of the requirements for the reproduction of capitalist relations of production," and doing this, in particular, through a system of prices corresponding to the requirements for this reproduction) fulfills a second function, this means, on the one hand, that *this function exists* and, therefore, that the *value-form and the price-form play an effective role;* but, on the other hand, it also means that this *function is modified,* in this very precise sense that, when the transition to socialism is carried out, *prices* can no longer be exclusively or even primarily determined by the *market* but must be determined by the *plan.*

To wish to "suppress" prices and money is to ignore the specific structure of the transitional economy, to ignore the relative independence of processes of production, and thus to ignore the functions that economic units still necessarily fulfill in so far as they are in possession of the means of production.

To refuse to subject prices to the requirements of the plan is likewise to ignore the structure of the transitional economy; it is to reject the intervention made by the property of the workers' state and, therefore, to leave the possession of the means of production to be transformed into property that is divided between the enterprises and, as a result, into property that cannot be owned by the immediate producers since the latter are then subjected to the requirements of reproduction of capitalist relations of production (which, for example, *will impose* such and such a change upon the level of employment and production).

Two essential points should be stressed here:

(1) The substitution of the criterion of *social and political effectiveness* for that of "profitability" indicates nothing other than the substitution of a *social economic calculation* (SEC) for a monetary calculation. Consequently, one of the objectives of SEC is to permit an *evaluation of the economic, social, and political effectiveness* of such and such a set of measures that are to be, or have already been, undertaken. For such an evaluation to have any meaning, it must be *independent of the system of prices* existing at a given moment since it will eventually have to be *used to modify existing prices and to establish new planned prices.*

(2) If, in principle, social economic calculation develops independently of the system of existing prices and enables a unified set of production and consumption objectives to be set up that are coherently interrelated and conform to political and social objectives, then the establishment—on the basis of this calculation—of a system of prices (which enables monetary calculation to be carried out) is none the less necessary since SEC, properly so called, can only be carried out on a "social scale." Yet, during the transitional period, the existence of production "enterprises" (and of economic units of consumption) signifies, on the one hand, that the processes of production and consumption develop in a relatively independent manner and, on the other hand, that the conditions in which these processes develop are relatively variable and difficult to predict "individually," although they can concomitantly be the object of aggregate statistical predictions. In order to enable enterprises and units of consumption to direct their activities in such a way that the latter develop in conformity with the plan (despite their relative independence), a system of prices is indispensable. This system must be *made known* to the agents who dominate the relatively independent processes; *under such conditions, these processes develop in a way that conforms best to the requirements of the plan.* This can be achieved, at least approximately, by a system of prices which are such that, when the agents who dominate particular production processes minimize their cost-prices, they can be certain that the techniques and means they put into operation are *politically and socially the most effective* without on each occasion having to

"consult" other units of production or economic institutions (which is practically impossible).

COMMENTS

To say that SEC (in opposition to monetary calculation) can only be carried out on a social scale does not mean that this calculation must intervene directly on a social formational scale (a country, for example). On the contrary, in practice, it seems necessary for there to be a combination (under the form of a superimposition) of calculations carried out within "social units of calculation" having a relatively reduced "size," and other calculations carried out on the scale of several of these units, up to a "level" that encompasses the totality of the social units of calculation. In effect, SEC requires that a direct comparison be undertaken between the various activities that are possible and actually substitutable as well as a comparison of possible social effects (including, of course, effects on the living and working conditions of the producers) of these activities and their combination. However, some of these comparisons are only internally significant within social units that have a relatively reduced "size," while other comparisons must be made on a larger scale, including comparisons at the level of the social formation in its general unity. Furthermore, calculations carried out at this final level only have meaning if they are dependent on the SEC made at the level of the various social units of calculation. The problems raised by these different types of calculation will have to be investigated in a subsequent text.

What has been stated here signifies, on the one hand, that *the value-form is utilized to influence production,* that is, to influence those aspects of production that cannot be the object of an immediate social direction and, on the other hand, that the *law of value* (in the strict sense) does not "regulate" production as it does through "market prices." [13]

It follows from the preceding analysis that the existence of a *system of planned prices* and of the *economic, ideological, and political preconditions* for this system to be observed and play a real role, leads to the appearance of a *second form of monetary calculation.* Here it really is a question of a "calculation in prices" that apparently does develop in the same way as a "calculation in prices" given by the market. However, because prices are not "given by the market" but are *fixed by the plan,* the "calculation in prices" (although carried out in terms of money) refers not solely to *commodity relations* but to *planned relations.* If these planned relations and the planned prices that correspond to them are the result of an economic calculation, then the monetary calculations carried out *on the basis of these planned prices* and the *objectives of the plan* are, in reality, *indirect economic calculations,* that is to say, calculations which, while being made in money, are clearly *economic calculations.*

In my book, *La Transition vers l'économie socialiste,* I pointed out a number of conditions under which a system of planned prices can be established that corresponds to the criterion of *social and political effectiveness.* Without a doubt, many of the things I said there need to be corrected and developed more fully, and this will have to be done in a subsequent text; in this text, my object has been to clarify, more adequately than I was able to in *La Transition,* the *nature* of different *types of calculation* and their relation to the *structures* of transitional social formations. I will now return to this question.

Notes

1. On this point, see Louis Althusser, "The Object of Capital," in *Reading Capital,* particularly pp. 175–79; and Etienne Balibar, "On the Basic Concepts of Historical Materialism," in the same book.
2. As we know, Marx defined the task of science as being precisely that of the reduction of the visible movement to the real internal movement: "It is a work of science to resolve the visible, merely external movement to the real internal movement." (*Capital,* 3:313)
3. Marx, *The Civil War in France,* p. 172.
4. It is essential to stress again, here, that the expression, "state ownership," or "state property," refers to the regulatory power exerted over the means

of production by political power; it does not imply that this political power is exercised through centralized institutions. The Paris Commune and the people's communes in China provide us with examples of such a "noncentralized" form of state property.

5. Here I am taking up a number of the propositions put forward in *La Transition vers l'économie socialiste*, but I am formulating them more precisely.

6. Marx, *Civil War*, pp. 172–73.

7. Ibid., p. 73. (The Chinese edition renders "cooperative associations" as "cooperative societies."—Trans.)

8. On this problem of prices, see chapter 6 of my work, *La Transition vers l'économie socialiste*.

9. Josef Stalin, *Economic Problems of Socialism in the USSR*, p. 21.

10. Ibid., p. 22.

11. The Chinese edition of *Economic Problems* renders "profitability" as "profitableness"; consequently, I have used the French edition here; see part 1, chapter 2, note 29—Trans.

12. Stalin, *Economic Problems*, p. 24.

13. On this point, see *La Transition*, p. 241.

Chapter 4

The structures of the processes of production, money, and the plan

We know that the transition between capitalism and socialism is characterized not by a relatively strict articulation of the production processes but by the relative independence of a considerable number of these processes. Because of this, a part of the means of production cannot be distributed a priori between the economic units of production and consumption in such a way that it is socially effective; the independence of the processes also results in the intervention of *money* in this process of distribution, which is itself an integral part of the social process of *reproduction*. When money intervenes in the relations between economic units, these units can "acquire" particular products in relation to the needs appropriate to production processes carried out within them, and also, therefore, at the very moment when these products are necessary for them.

In the transitional period, the structure of the processes of production and the social conditions of their articulation explain why the means of production, even when they are the object of an a priori distribution, can have a *price* that is not in the least "fictitious," since the economic units must either actually "pay" this price (even when products are assigned to them via distribution) or account for it in their calculations of cost-price, depreciation, etc. In the absence of a system of significant prices (that is, a system that corresponds to the conditions of production and the requirements of planning), no *social control by the enterprises over the use of the products of labor* would be possible, and this would render planning itself impossible. When the system of prices is *in general use,* and when these prices are actually *paid,* then there exists a *money that fulfills the function of a general equivalent.* Furthermore, this function of general equivalent can only be *potential.* This occurs, for example, every time economic organizations impose a set of *rules* that limit or specify the uses to which the economic units can put their available sums of money.

Generally, it can be said that these rules aim at ensuring that the role of *confirmation* of the social character of labor played by the *sale* of a product coincides as closely as possible with the *anticipatory* role of this social character, which is played by the economic plan. To the extent that the plan fulfills its anticipatory function, labor is not only *social* labor but, according to Marx's expression, *socialized labor.* This term indicates the fact that labor is to be carried out under the control of associated producers.

In contrast to the function of (at least potential) *general equivalent* that money fulfills between the economic units, is the function of *accounting category* performed by money in the relations between the "technical units" (for example, between the different "workshops" or "departments" of the same factory). The expression, "technical units" (see above, part 2, chapter 2) has been chosen because the "splitting up" of an economic unit into "technical units" occurs primarily on the basis of technical determinations. Yet, this "splitting up" *also* has *social determinations:* in actual fact, it can *vary* according to the dominant ideological and political relations. It can, for example, be a means for consolidating either the domination of the producers or nonproducers over the division of labor in the economic unit. Thus, the "technical units" primarily fulfill technical functions (functions of material production), but they also perform functions that are political (functions of direction) and ideological. Consequently, the conditions under which they are split up are far from being "purely" technical.

In the relations between technical units belonging to the same economic unit, the principal function of money is one of accounting. This accountancy does not result in the intervention of "effective" prices, i.e., thus giving rise to payments. Money, here, is in every way *imaginary;* it cannot bring about payments; it is not an "instrument" that confirms the social character of labor.

Under these conditions, in interworkshop relations, prices are essentially the expression of costs of social labor, costs whose conditions of assessment have been established socially.

COMMENTS

To say that the prices of products circulating between the technical units of the same economic unit are the expression of *social labor costs* means they are no longer the simple "translation into money terms" of the *actual* labor costs that have been required to obtain different products but something much more complex (as in the value of products itself), which can only be evaluated by taking into account the interrelation between different types of production and their *concrete social effects.*[1] To the extent that these prices are not "given" by the market but are the result of social evaluations that correspond to the requirements of an economic politics concretized through planning, prices are no longer entirely "prices"; nevertheless, they are still *partly* so by the very fact that they are "expressed" in money.

At the level of technical units, "prices" are, therefore, essentially instruments of accounting, since the production of these different units is not determined at the level of the unit; this determination constitutes one of the *functions of direction* of the economic unit.

COMMENTS

The necessity for a "direction" is objectively inscribed in the *co-operation* of the laborers participating in the ensemble of processes that take place within a given economic unit. Depending upon the dominant political and ideological relations, this directing function can be taken up *by different social agencies* (director, directing committee, revolutionary committee, etc.). Such an agency is responsible for *coordinating* labor processes in the economic unit and for "representing" the unit vis-à-vis other economic units and institutions. As a result, this agency plays an *active role in the articulation of* the production processes "external to" this economic unit.

It is this *double function* of *internal* direction and *external* articulation that is presented under the form of "administration." The latter is always subordinated to external social requirements, which are either those of the "market" or those of the "plan." Within the framework of planning, this *subordination* has a *directly political* character, the plan being the concrete expression of an economic politics.

The function of direction of an *enterprise* is not "imposed" by itself; it is only ensured if particular conditions are given: in the first place, a particular *structure of the labor processes,* which makes the enterprise an effective (simple or complex) economic unit, and, secondly, particular political and ideological relations through which *authority,* that is, the *power* of direction, is imposed.

When, during the transitional period, the power to direct an enterprise is ineffective, the functioning of money in intereconomic unit relations can even corrupt intertechnical unit relations (for example, following changes in the direction of products, external sales, etc.).

That such effects can be produced confirms the function of *potential general equivalent* that money performs. Even within the enterprise, this political function can become effective when the power to direct the enterprises is no longer secure.

In the relations between economic units, instances in which there is a break in socially imposed limitations on money's function as a general equivalent can objectively be more frequent precisely because, at this level, money is called upon to intervene constantly as a *means of payment,* because of the very nature of the relations that are established between economic units.

An additional problem posed in social formations in transition between capitalism and socialism is to ensure that *money is confined within the limits of those functions which must be its own.* Lack of respect for these limits, in effect, risks leading to the complete *autonomy* of economic units, that is, to their nonsubordination to the plan.

When the intervention of money is still necessary for the functioning of the economy, the contradiction between "money" and the "plan" only constitutes one of the *forms* within which the contradiction between *market relations* and *planned relations,* and also, therefore, the contradiction between the law of value and the law of social direction of the economy, is made manifest.

As we have seen earlier, it is a question here of an objective contradiction; nothing is served by "denying" this contradiction, and it is futile to want to "abolish" it by, for example, suppressing the monetary operations between state enterprises. Such a suppression would only lead to an increase in the "opacity" of the economy since the functions of money would continue to be carried out under different forms, but these could no longer be either identified or dominated; by refusing to see these contradictions, one would have driven them into a "parallel economic world."

Thus, the real problem is to determine objectively what, at each moment, taking into account the state of the productive forces and the *ensemble of social relations,* are *the conditions under which it is possible to confine money within the functions that it can fulfill in contributing to the realization of the plan.* To examine this problem, we would have to go beyond the limits of our present research. Yet, it is essential to stress that, because of the very structure of transitional social formations, these conditions depend, *at one and the same time,* upon the political level (for example, the modalities and the quality of the control exercised over institutions responsible for monetary functions), on the *forms* of intervention of this level in the economic level (for example, a correct planning of prices and supplies), and on the ideological level (discipline, honesty, sense of public interest, etc.).

The *effective* intervention of money in the relations between economic subjects shows that it is not sufficient to say, as Stalin did in the text cited previously, that the state "distributes the means of production" between the productive economic units. In fact, as we have seen, it generally *distributes money as well,* as often as not through the medium of the budget and the banking system. With this *money,* the economic units can buy the means of production—primarily, the objects of labor *that they need*—and, in principle, can adapt the *quality* of these means and the *moment* at which they purchase them to their own needs.

Consequently, the intervention of money and of commodity categories is not in the least "imaginary" nor due only to "accounting." It has *effects,* and this is because this intervention is *imposed by the structure of the processes of production.* This structure is such that a *direct distribution in kind* of the means and objects of labor would not generally be reconcilable with a *socially effective* utilization of these means of production.

We have just said that the productive economic units can "in principle" adapt the *quality* of products they buy and the *moment* at which they purchase them to their own productive needs; we said "in principle," because, in the practice of many transitional social formations, it has been considered possible to substitute the decisions of organizations external to the economic units for the decisions made by those who direct these units. This often leads to *a situation in which deliveries made to the units of production are no longer adapted to the needs of these units,* without such a situation being politically necessary.

One result of this is, in effect, that the planning agencies institute an a priori distribution of the objects of labor (they then carry out functions that depend upon *administration*); another result is that in relation to the circulation of commodities, these agencies add additional rules for distribution over and above those that relate to planning (for example, allocating the use of particular products, priority in assigning particular means of production to particular factories, etc.).

It is clearly false to confuse the imposition of distribution regulations with an objective transformation of the articulation of production processes—a transformation that could permit the value-form to disappear. In fact, the use of distribution regulations, if it originates from *disequilibriums* between available quantities and needs, that is, from "shortages" or "maladjustments," very often objectively reveals *the consequences of the noncoordination* of production processes. *Regulation has as its aim here to limit the effects of a noncoordination* that exceeds the *limits* within which *money* can fulfill its functions *in keeping with* the imperatives of the *plan.*

Moreover, it must be stressed that state regulation is only one of the possible modes of a socially satisfactory distribution of products available in relatively insufficient quantities. It is a mode of existence that is "externally" imposed on the economic units and that ultimately implies recourse to *legal sanctions.*

There is another modality of distribution that presupposes the development of socialist ideological relations. It is formed by the *cooperation of units of production,* a cooperation which has as its object the fullest social realization of a set of economic and political objectives. Such cooperation ensures the "socialist interdependence" of the units of production (this interdependence, therefore, is neither strictly "technical" nor "economic"). It seems that the generalization of such cooperation corresponds to a new "stage," which is character- ized by the retreat of the operational field of money and state intervention and thus by an *extension of the operational field of immediate producers* through their domination over the conditions of production and reproduction.

Generally, in the first stage of the transition, the existence of regulatory measures that are superimposed concomitantly on the plan and on money testifies to the frailty of *social domination* over the general unity of the processes of production. It is this frailty that makes it necessary for the socialist state to oppose, *through regulatory measures,* the extension of the operational field of commodity catego- ries. If such a regulation did not exist, the role of commodity relations between units of production would increase so that the activity of these units would correspond less and less to the requirements of the plan and more and more to the requirements of the law of value.

However, it is clear that, *beyond a certain degree of maladjustment between the various processes of production, no regulatory measures can be effective any longer; when this is the case, it is the objective economic disequilibriums themselves that must be reduced.* The refusal to recognize this necessity can lead to a more or less profound disorganization of the economy and eventually to futile attempts to "abolish money"—this

abolition being made in every way "responsible" for the disequilibriums that it simply brings to the surface.

This confirms what we said earlier: legal property ownership of the
means of production by the state is not sufficient to ensure social unity
or the social coordination of the processes of production. It is for this
reason that the disappearance of commodity relations depends upon
particularly complex transformations.

As we stressed earlier, this disappearance, far from being accompanied by economic calculation, must, on the contrary, permit the
development of a real social economic calculation. This calculation is,
at one and the same time, the condition and the effect of a total control
by the laborers over their means of production and over the results of
their labor. It seems to me that, by taking this into account, the
analysis of the different forms of economic and monetary calculation
can, and must, be undertaken.

Notes

1. On this point, see *La Transition vers l'économie socialiste*, pp. 236–40.

General bibliography

Althusser, Louis, and Balibar, Etienne. *Reading Capital.* Translated by Ben Brewster. New York: Pantheon, 1970; London: New Left Books, 1970.

Althusser, Louis; Balibar, Etienne; and Establet, R. *Lire le Capital.* Paris: Maspero, 1965.

Bettelheim, Charles. *Planification et croissance accélérée.* Paris: Maspero, 1967.

———. *Studies in the Theory of Planning.* Translated by Brian Pearce. Bombay: 1959, and Hakibbutz Hameuchad, Israel: 1963.

———. *La Transition vers l'économie socialiste.* Paris: Maspero, 1968.

Brus, Wlodzimierz. *The Market in a Socialist Economy.* London: 1972.

Engels, Friedrich. *Anti-Dühring.* Moscow: Progress Publishers, 1969; Paris: Editions Sociales, 1950.

Kosygin, Aleksei. *New Methods of Economic Management in the USSR.* Plenary meeting of the CPSU central committee, 27–29 September. Moscow: Novoski Press Agency, 1965.

Lenin, V. I. "The Immediate Tasks of the Soviet Government." *Collected Works,* 27:235–75. Moscow: Progress Publishers, n.d.

———. "The Draft Programme of the R.C.P.(B)." *Collected Works,* 29:119–25.

———. *Workers' Control and the Nationalization of Industry.* Moscow: Progress Publishers, 1968.

Mao Tse-tung. "On the Policy Concerning Industry and Commerce." *Selected Works:* 4. Peking: Foreign Languages Press, 1969.

———. "Report to the Second Plenary Session of the Seventh Central Committee of the Communist Party of China." *Selected Works:* 4. Peking: Foreign Languages Press, 1969.

———. *On the Correct Handling of Contradictions Among the People.* Peking: Foreign Languages Press, 1966.

Marx, Karl, and Engels, Friedrich. *Critique of the Gotha Programme.* Peking: Foreign Languages Press, 1972.

Nove, A. *The Soviet Economy: An Introduction.* London: Allen & Unwin, 1965.

Preobrazhensky, E. *The New Economics*. London and New York: Oxford University Press, 1965.

Stalin, J. *Economic Problems of Socialism in the USSR*. Peking: Foreign Languages Press, 1972.

Supplementary bibliography

Ganczer. "Planification globale et planification sectorale." *Economie appliquée* XX (1967): 23–46.

Hinton, William. *Fanshen*. New York: Vintage, 1966.

Laszlo, I. "La planification dans le nouveau système de gestion économique en Hongrie." *Economie Appliquée* XX (1967): 7–22.

Liontiev, I. "Plan et méthodes économiques de direction." *Recherches internationales à la lumière du marxisme*, May–June 1965, pp. 118–22.

Liberman, E. "Plan, bénéfice et prime." *Recherches internationales à la lumière du marxisme*, May–June 1965, pp. 27–35.

Marchisio, Hélène. "Les campagnes chinoises au lendemain de la réforme agraire." *Arch. Int. de Soc. de la Coop. et du Dév.*, no. 20, July–December 1966 (Collège Coopératif, 7, av. Franco-Russe, Paris).

———. "Réforme agraire et organisation coopératives en Chine de 1927 à 1962." In the same journal, above, July–December 1967.

———. "La contradiction, moteur du developpement dans une commune populaire chinoise. Enquête sur la Brigade de Dazhai." In the same journal, above, January–June 1968.

Meyer, M. "L'application de la réforme de l'entreprise." *Annuaire de l'URSS* (1967): 231–66.

Nemtchinov, V. "Gestion et planification sociale de la production en URSS." *Recherches internationales à la lumière du marxisme*, May–June 1965, pp. 36–54.

Richman. "La formulation des plans opérationnels d'entreprise dans l'industrie soviétique." *Soviet Studies*, July 1963.

Robinson, Joan. *The Cultural Revolution in China*. London: Penguin Books, 1969.

Schroder, Gertrud E. "Soviet Economic 'Reforms.' A Study in Contradiction." *Soviet Studies*, July 1968, pp. 1–20.

Wilcsek, J. "The Role of Profit in the Management of Enterprises." *Acta Oeconomica* II (1967): 63–76.

Zaleski, E. "Les réformes de la planification en URSS." *Cahiers de l'I.S.E.A.*, June 1964, pp. 3–96.

———. "Les réformes d'Octobre 1965 et la gestion de l'entreprise en URSS." *Cahiers de l'I.S.E.A.*, May 1966, pp. 133–78.

Zielinski, J. *On the Theory of Socialist Planning.* London: Oxford University Press, 1968.